I Will Lie Down in Peace

I Will Lie Down in Peace

USHA JESUDASAN

PARTRIDGE
A Penguin Random House Company

To order additional copies of this book, contact
Partridge India
000 800 10062 62
orders.india@partridgepublishing.com

www.partridgepublishing.com/india

I will lie down and sleep in peace,
for you alone, O Lord,
make me dwell in safety.

Psalm 4:8

Acknowledgments

My deep gratitude to:

The Faith and Healing Cell, Vellore, who saw the need for Kumar's story to be written and shared, and who gave me a small grant to enable me to write it.

My very special thanks to:

My friend, Asha Nehemiah, who edited the manuscript so painstakingly, and gave many valuable suggestions. Helen Jothi, for all her help in typing the manuscript. Emma and Tharyan Koshi for taking care of me in every way.

Anna Zachariah, whose arms, heart and home were always open to me.

Dr. P. Zachariah, without whose constant encouragement and faith in me, especially at times when I was ready to give up, this book would never have been completed.

My parents, Amala and Dr Emmanuel for all their love and care over the years.

My first publishers, EastWest Books (Madras) Pvt. Ltd for their appreciation of our story, and their willingness to publish it and to donate the proceeds from this book for leprosy work.

My deepest appreciation and gratitude to:

James and John and Mallika.

Kumar's story quickly became a family project. James and John read every line almost as it was being written and relived the whole experience and shared their memories and insights of this time, despite the great pain it brought them.

Mallika understood that Appa's book was something special, and would play quietly beside me, never disturbing me.

To my children, James, John and Mallika, I offer this book with great love, and the hope that the lessons we learned during this painful time will never be forgotten or allowed to go waste.

Usha Jesudasan

Contents

1. A Journey Beyond Our Dreams 1
2. Finding A Life Partner 6
3. Choose You This Day Whom You Will Serve 13
4. Life In Karigiri 23
5. The Dreadful Secret 37
6. Our Days In Singapore 42
7. An Unexpected Gift 51
8. A Traumatic Awakening 56
9. Tears, Turmoil And Glimpses Of Joy 66
10. The Second Coma 76
11. The Valley Of The Shadow Of Death 90
12. An Act Of Defiance 105
13. In Acceptance Lies Peace 111
14. Epilogue 160

1. A Journey Beyond Our Dreams

October 29th, 1996, was to be a special day for us. My husband, Dr Kumar Jesudasan, was to leave for Vietnam that day. But events did not take him to Vietnam—but instead thrust him, and us, into another journey, way beyond any of our dreams.

Trips to other countries were not unusual for Kumar. Over a period of ten years, he had travelled to about thirty different countries in Asia, Africa, Europe and the Pacific, with one purpose, to fulfill the ruling passion of his life—to reduce and some day put an end to the sufferings caused by leprosy.

The Vietnam visit was special in that it was his first journey not only to that country but also to the mainland of East Asia. Before such a trip to a new place, we usually read up all we could about it and familiarized ourselves with the places he would visit and the local customs. Sometimes, we even got him to learn phrases like 'good morning,' and 'thank you' in the local language. The Vietnamese language was a tongue-twister and he planned to get by with a few words in French.

"Have you finished your shopping lists?" he asked the boys, the previous evening.

Jamie, tall and lanky at fourteen, was almost his father's height. He loved loud music, striking T-shirts and had a passion for shoes. "Pick up some new music for me please, Appa, and a pair of shoes if you can," he said.

John, at ten, was a quieter child. Saying goodbye to his father was always a traumatic experience for him, and so he just hung around Kumar, wanting nothing more than just to be beside him for as long as he could.

"What can I bring for my little John-John?" said Kumar, drawing the little boy into his arms and using the affectionate name he had given him as a baby. "Nothing, Appa. I just want you back safe," John replied snuggling his tear-stained face into his father's warm neck.

The evening passed by in getting his things ready and in last minute 'don't forget' instructions from me. Later, there was a meal with some friends and Kumar was his normal self though he seemed rather tired.

Actually, for some months now, Kumar had been getting tired by the evening, as though a normal day was too much for him. Our family and many of his colleagues were not too happy about another lengthy journey for him at this time. His long-standing diabetes was reason enough. We would rather not think of the more dreaded malady, cirrhosis of the liver, which we knew would claim him one day. At the age of forty-six, and with so many plans still ahead of him, this seemed like a distant nightmare.

Very early the next morning, I was woken by noises from the bathroom. The sound of coughing and retching did not seem normal, so I quickly slipped out of bed and found Kumar sitting on the bathroom floor looking pale and very unwell.

"I don't think you should go on this trip, sweetheart," I said, and even as I spoke I realized that he was too sick to hear what I was saying.

The obvious thing to do was to check his blood sugar. I called Dr Selvashekar, Kumar's young friend and colleague on the campus of the Schieffelin Leprosy Research and Training Centre at Karigiri, where we lived. Kumar's blood sugar, the most likely factor to cause trouble, was normal, yet something else was wrong as he seemed to be losing consciousness.

We rushed him to the Christian Medical College Hospital at Vellore, 17 kilometres away, where Kumar had studied and trained to be a doctor many years earlier.

Although Kumar was unconscious, he was thrashing around and groaning as if in severe pain. One look at Kumar, and his physician, Dr George Kurian, said, "This is serious, Usha, it is a hepatic coma. He has become unconscious due to liver failure. The liver is the major organ which disposes of the toxic products of the body mechanisms. Usually, such toxins are excreted through the kidneys. They are also neutralised within the body itself. The liver detoxifies these products and protects the body. In advanced liver failure these toxic substances begin to accumulate and it has now reached a point where Kumar's brain has been affected. That's why he is in a coma. Although he seems so inert, his brain is actually malfunctioning—hence the screams and the thrashing around. Usually it takes a patient about seventy-two hours to recover with anti-coma regimen, as I hope he will. But for the moment, all we can do is wait and see."

Kumar was placed in the intensive care unit (ICU). There was nothing to do but wait. It seemed that at that moment my whole world caved in. My mind was numb for a while.

"O Lord, what is happening to us? Please be with Kumar and bring him back to us safely," I prayed.

Sitting there, in the icy atmosphere of the intensive care unit, it all seemed so unreal. Covered with a deathly white sheet, his hands and feet were tied up with restrainers. Restrainers are flat wads of cloth and elastic by which a patient's hands and feet are tied to the railings of the bed, to prevent him from thrashing about and hurting himself. Spread-eagled and tied up this way, the man on the bed looked so unlike my Kumar. His hands felt heavy and cold. I had always remembered them as soft and warm and reassuring. His eyes were closed and there was no response from him at all. He could neither see, nor feel anything, nor hear. I was allowed to sit beside him and hold his hands for a while. Convinced that he could still hear my voice, I bent down to his ear and reminded him of the things we used to do, of how much I loved him, of how much I needed him. Pouring out all our hopes for the future, I told him to wake up soon. But there was no response. Only the flashes and bleeps of the monitor to which he was plugged told me that his heart was functioning and that his blood pressure was normal.

Not being able to bear this anymore, I went outside. The corridor outside the ICU was deserted. As there was nowhere to sit, I sat down on the cold, grey stone floor in utter disbelief. It was about six in the morning. Dawn was just breaking and the first rays of the sun began to pierce their beams through the dark skies. For the first time, I thought about what this could mean for us and I began to cry. Almost two decades of loving and sharing, of being together and building a home had made me take it all for granted. Now, faced suddenly with the prospect of losing it all, I was terrified at the thought of the frightening loneliness looming over me.

2. Finding A Life Partner

My mind went back to the time when, as a young girl, much of my thoughts turned to love and marriage. It would have to be somebody rich and handsome and, of course, someone who loved me to bits. Someone who matched my passion for life, music, people and fashion. Someone with a sense of humour.

My father was a doctor, a specialist in chest diseases, and my mother a primary school teacher. We lived in the U.K., in a small village in south-east England called Benenden. Our activities at the weekends and holidays centred around the local community and church. I was a Queen's Guide with responsibilities that varied from visiting the elderly who lived alone, to making sure that the brass crosses in the church were cleaned for Sunday services. Though I had grown up in England, my parents saw to it that all our values regarding family, duty and commitment to marriage, were Indian. Afraid that I would get lost and seduced by English values, which were so different from our own, they watched over my activities and social life with care.

Soon after my twenty-first birthday, I graduated with an honours degree in Philosophy and Education and got a job teaching English. It was a well paid job with excellent living accommodation and plenty of perks. The single life suited me as I enrolled in evening classes to enrich my life, made new friends and lived away from home with a new found freedom.

It didn't thrill my parents in the same way. There were anxious letters going back and forth within the larger family in India, regarding suitable young men. None of them appealed to me and by the end of the year I began to despair if there would ever be anyone to suit me.

That summer my mother and I made a trip to India to attend a favourite cousin's wedding. It was the marriage season and we were invited to several society weddings.

On one such occasion, dressed in a very pretty green sari, I was looking forward to a happy evening. Half way through, I was told that there was a nice young man called Kumar Jesudasan who wanted to meet me. So we had to leave.

Kumar was a young doctor from a traditional Tamil family, who was looking for a bride. The elders in both our families thought we would be well suited. At our first meeting, Kumar was just as nervous as I was. After a brief introduction, we were left alone to discuss 'things that mattered.'

"Do you always look like this?" were his first words to me.

I was embarrassed thinking that perhaps my eye make-up had smudged or that my lipstick was the wrong colour.

Sensing my confusion, he tried to put me at ease by saying, "What I meant was, do you always wear so much make-up? And do you always wear your hair like that?"

"Oh yes, it's part of my personality. Actually, my hair is dead straight, so I spent the whole afternoon curling it so that it could fall like this onto my shoulders. Don't you like it?"

There was no reply. Then he looked at my nails. Long and polished a bright red. Cheekily, I fluttered my eyelashes at him. By now I realized that the colour and attempted glamour did not appeal to him. If I was going to blow it, I might as well do it properly I thought, and explained that my nails were real, but my eyelashes were not, and I peeled them off for him to see. Kumar, decently and politely, I thought, hid his horror quite well.

Just then, something warm and wet touched my feet. It was the most enormous frog I had ever seen. I shoved it off and resumed our conversation. After a few minutes, it was back, hopping again in my direction. The only way to avoid the frog was to move closer to Kumar. As I inched closer, the frog hopped nearer. I could see Kumar's amused gaze as he sat there and wondered just how close I would come. Finally, gallantly he kicked the frog away.

We spoke of his commitment to leprosy work, his life as a Christian, his duty to his widowed mother, and of both our general likes and dislikes. Several times that evening, he made me laugh.

But there was one aspect of me that he had not seen. Due to polio as a child, I had a noticeable limp. Several times I had eavesdropped into conversations where I heard, "Many good men won't want a girl with a limp." Hurt and upset, I had decided that whoever wanted to marry me should do so despite the limp. Kumar had not been told about the limp, so he had to see it for himself.

We walked along the road to my uncle's house where I was staying, and I was nervous. So far I had liked his ways and his manner. Would he be put off by the limp? He noticed it and asked me about it.

"Does it bother You?" I asked.

Sensing,my anxiety, he held my hands for the first time and said, " No, Usha, it doesn't bother me at all," and smiled into my eyes. I too smiled happily back at him. "But all this make-up does," he grinned.

We were engaged a few days later with the understanding that we would have a year to get to know each other while Kumar did his Diploma in Tropical Medicine and Public Health in London.

That year was exciting and exasperating. I discovered that Kumar, with his highly evangelical Christian background, did not approve of my "frivolous" ways of dressing. For a while, I dressed as a plain Jane. I wore a dull blue or some pale colour to please him. I grew my hair long, I even cut my nails and wore a plain varnish. But I wasn't happy doing it.

"It's not that I actually mind," Kumar said one day. "In fact, you look very sweet, but I have a certain image back home and all my friends would be horrified to think I married someone like you."

Sweet…someone like you…these words stung me.

"Hang your friends!" I said, and burst into tears.

That night we had our first big disagreement. Neither of us was going to give in. Too much was at stake for both of us. For him, his reputation, and for me, a large part of my personality.

"You do realize you are going to be a missionary wife, don't you? You will look so out of place in Karigiri. People will look at you and get the wrong impression."

It all fell on deaf ears. He appealed to my mother.

"You have to accept her as she is, Kumar'" was her advice.

We agreed not to spoil our relationship by squabbling about it all the time. Meanwhile, there was another growing area of concern for me. Kumar expected me to accompany him on his speaking assignments to raise funds for The Leprosy Mission in London. This was very hard for me as it involved looking like a young missionary wife, sitting in cold rooms, talking to those who raised funds, and generally being very religious and sober. Kumar was so earnest when he preached or spoke, it was obvious his faith and his work were very important to him.

I seriously considered returning the beautiful engagement ring he had given me for I felt I wasn't cut out for the role of being a missionary wife. Our relationship which was passionate and loving suddenly became undefined with all the growing pressures. Sometimes we parted in silence. But always with the secret hope that the other person would change.

Then I met Barbara Askew, the wife of the Secretary of The Leprosy Mission, who had been a missionary wife in India herself for many years. Barbara shared with me some of her experiences of being a missionary wife living away from home in a distant land.

"The men always have their work cut out for them, the wives have no defined role. You will have to build a home that is happy, comfortable and a model for others as well as being the rock on which Kumar can lean." She spoke too of the dedication, the commitment and the love that was required between two people to make a marriage work. "God wants you as you are, Usha," she said, "There is no ideal image that you need to be. In fact, there is no image. Just be yourself."

To Kumar she said, "God loves colour and beauty just as much as anyone else, for He created them. You and Usha need to be a team, you cannot do this kind of work on your own. You need to pray whether it is God's Will for you to be together and to serve Him in whatever way you can, and not worry about whether Usha will fit the mould that everyone expects of her." Wise words of advice for which we were both thankful.

For Kumar's part, in a moving letter to me, he copied out part of Christina Rossetti's poem.

"Yet while I love my God the most, I deem

That I can never love You over much;

I love Him more, so let me love you too;

Yea as I apprehend it, love is such

I cannot love you if I love not Him,

I cannot love Him, if I love not you."

We were married in Madras, in the midst of our families and friends. To many who saw us that day we seemed lovely but mismatched. Kumar was the son of James K. Jesudasan, a well known industrialist with a reputation for charm and generosity, and his wife Nancy. Mr. Jesudasan died while Kumar was still in medical school and much of the responsibility of looking after his mother fell onto his shoulders. He was a highly evangelical Christian, a doctor committed to serving those suffering from leprosy, a very old-fashioned young man, and here he was, marrying a fancy girl from a western background.

Late on our wedding night, still dressed in my sari of sparkling white and gold, with the fragrant garland of white lilies around my neck, I promised Kumar that we would not allow the differences in our personalities and upbringing to get in the way of our love for each other. For we believed, with all our heart, that love would overcome all our apprehensions and glue us together in the right places. Kumar responded by kissing the finger on which he had placed my wedding ring only hours earlier, and whispered the same words, he had used in reply to the toast at the reception, "With God as our guide, and you by my side, it will be an exciting life to look forward to."

Here I was so many years later, still at his side, but utterly helpless and forlorn now.

3. Choose You This Day Whom You Will Serve

The narrow corridor outside the intensive care unit is usually empty, but this evening there was a crowd. A large group of men and women stood outside, weeping. Somebody wanted to know if there was someone famous admitted inside."No, only our doctor," said one of the men.

Some of those waiting were overwrought with anxiety and just barged into the ICU to enquire about Kumar. The nurses promptly scolded them and chased them away. But they were not to be deterred. They waited for hours. The nurse on duty saw me sitting beside Kumar and told me, "Please send them away. They are blocking the passage."

I sighed. How could I expect this young girl who was so proper and efficient to understand what Kumar meant to this ragged bunch of people? I left Kumar for a while and went outside to share their pain. So many hands reached out to me, hands that were worn out, hands that were no hands at all, hands that were clawed and twisted. As I touched each one, I remembered how it all started...... and how they all came to be here at this time.

Their relationship with Kumar actually began long before I knew him myself, and went back almost twenty years to when he had just qualified as a doctor. Kumar had joined the Schieffelin Leprosy Research and Training Centre at Karigiri for a short stint, with no intention of staying on. He was posted in the department of Epidemiology and Leprosy Control.

Every morning, a medical team consisting of a doctor, a nurse, a physiotherapist, a pharmacist und a cobbler from Karigiri, would visit the villages to examine and treat leprosy patients. These clinics were held in the open air under the shade of large trees. Kumar didn't know much about leprosy, but he was learning. The paramedical staff who worked in the field areas took an instant liking to this young doctor with the kind and genial manner. He was eager to learn from them and often cycled or rode his motorbike with them after working hours to get the feel of what leprosy work was really like. He found it arduous and tiring, travelling in areas where there were often no roads. Long mornings of sitting in the sun, listening to story after story of pain and misery, of rejection and fear. His medical college days at the Christian Medical College Hospital, Vellore, were now behind him and he looked forward to an exciting career as a doctor, preferably in America. Until then, he put his heart into the work assigned to him each day in Karigiri.

It had been one such busy morning, an especially hectic one without a break, with the paramedical worker lining up patients to be examined at the successive village clinics. Kumar and his team finally relaxed after the last patient turned to go home. They lounged under the shady trees, enjoying the coconut water provided by a grateful patient. This was the last clinic of the day, and they were all looking forward to going home, when there was an interruption.

"Sir, there is one more patient. He has come late, an old man. Please have a look at him, he is one of our most difficult patients."

Wrapped up in a tattered old blanket stood the most pitiful specimen of a human being Kumar had ever seen. Hands that were clawed like a bird just about managed to curl around a stout stick. The old man's face was like untanned leather. Coarse, nut-coloured and withered. His nose had sunk completely into his face giving him a misshapen frightening look. Bare feet were covered with a grimy bandage stained yellow with pus. Weary eyes which stared at this new doctor suddenly turned defiant. They seemed to say, "So, what are you going to do about me?"

Kumar bent down and undid the bandage. Waves of disgust and nausea swept over him. The foot was almost worn out. There was no skin, the flesh was pink in places, but mostly yellow with oozing pus. Kumar shrank away at the sight. It was his first look at a badly ulcerated leprosy foot. As he probed the wound in what was left of the flesh, Kumar saw something which he had never seen before. Maggots. He squatted down by the man's foot and began to pull the maggots out one by one. Wriggling, squirming, fat little worms, trying to find shelter from the probes. Kumar settled down to pull them all out. As each one was pulled out, he held up the wriggling thing for a moment until the paramedical worker counted it and then flung it away into the dust.

"Sir, this man always comes in this state. Each time, we clean him up, give him new sandals and send him home to rest, but still he comes back in this state. What are we to do with him?"

Kumar turned to the old man, "See how much time I've spent on you. Do you think I have nothing better to do? Do you think I enjoyed pulling these things out from your leg? Go home and rest. Next time you come back to the clinic in this state, I won't treat you and finally we will have to cut your leg off. Is that what you want?"

The man remained passive and immobile. He didn't utter a single word throughout the whole procedure. He just looked on with helpless eyes that seemed to say to Kumar, "You don't understand at all, young doctor. You say go home.....but I have no home. you say rest.....but for men like me there is no rest. We are chased away from every place we go to. And if I sat in one place and rested like you say, who would feed me? We have no hope, no future, no dreams like you, young doctor."

The team sped away again in the van and stopped for a meal at a nearby hotel. Kumar could not stomach the idea of food, for the putrid smell of decaying flesh and the memory of pulling out the maggots still haunted him. Hungry now, he was angry with the old man for messing up his appetite. On the way home, he asked about this patient. His name was Mani and he was a beggar. He slept in temple sanctuaries and under the trees. He ate whatever was offered to the gods or whatever someone threw him out of pity. He had no home, no family, no job. Leprosy had stolen them all away from him.

That night as he lay on his bed, Kumar could not sleep. It was hot and airless in the room and he put his sleeplessness down to the heat. Every now and then, images of the old man flashed through his mind. The harsh words he had used earlier that day came back to haunt him. He got out of bed, restless and upset. Unable to sleep, he went out and sat down on the stone steps. The night air, cool and fragrant with the perfume of jasmine, heightened his sensitivity. The sky was cloudless and spangled with clusters of glittering stars. The serenity of this night-time beauty began to minister to him like a balm. The tightness in his heart lifted and his mind wandered over to the gospel story of Jesus healing the man with leprosy. A strong force compelled him to go in and read the passage in Matthew's gospel.

As he read, Kumar recreated the scene for himself. Jesus surrounded by throngs of people. Each one eager for his company, for his teaching, for his healing, for his touch, for his love. Then he saw Jesus tired. Jesus hungry. Jesus wanting the day to be over so that he could relax with his friends. Yet never turning anyone away. Never admonishing anyone who came to him for healing. Never laying down any conditions to those who came for succour. There in the middle of all this crowd, a man throws himself before Jesus. The others shrink back from him in horror, for the man has leprosy. The crowd looks on in amazement as Jesus stretches his hand out towards the man. He touches hands which are just stumps and caresses hollowed cheeks, like one would do to a favourite child. Jesus looks at him with all his Father's love and compassion and simply says, "Be clean." The man with leprosy is healed.

The images disappeared from Kumar's eyes. He was no longer in the crowd watching Jesus, but back in his little room in the Karigiri guest house.

"This is what I am supposed to do," thought Kumar. He was close enough to God to know that this was a special moment, a moment when God was speaking to him. To work with leprosy patients for the rest of his life was certainly not the kind of calling he expected or wanted. It was neither glamorous nor well paid. But nevertheless, a clear call it was. Without a doubt, he knew that God had touched his heart and life that day with a specific mission. To reach out, to touch and to heal those suffering from leprosy.

Kumar went out and sat under the wide canopy of stars again. The earlier restlessness had ceased and in its place was a sense of peace. A verse from the Bible came into his mind, "Choose you this day whom you will serve." God had given him a mission and a vision. Sitting on the grey stone steps outside the guest house, Kumar made his commitment to leprosy work, and to Karigiri.

He recounted much later, "At that point, I realized that Jesus was asking me to pick up my cross and follow him. All this while, I had professed to be a Christian, taking part in all the Christian activities in college. I had committed my life to serving God, wherever this may be, and I was pretty sure that it was to be in America. Now, God seemed to be saying, 'Let's see if you really mean it, Kumar. Choose now whom you will serve.' I knew it had to be a deliberate choice. God didn't want me to drift into it, to see if I liked it or to see what the future prospects were. He needed me to make a choice right then. No asking for advice, or what other people thought. No giving in to family pressure either. I thought of the great names in leprosy that I knew, Dr Brand, Dr Job, Dr Fritschi. They all lived such simple, sacrificial, almost frugal lives. Was I being called to follow in their footsteps? Could I possibly do it? The cross I had to pick up and bear would be the constant pull between the good life that tempted me and the vision I had been granted through the old man in the clinic."

He prayed a lot over this commitment and was completely at peace within himself. All his early desires of going to America had dissolved and he was happy knowing that his future was in God's hands. Armed with a new sense of calling, Kumar began his career in the department of Epidemiology in the Schieffelin Leprosy Research and Training Centre at Karigiri in 1975. He felt that the call that he had had, the strange encounter with the old man with the ulcer, was a form of guidance. God had chosen His own way of communicating to Kumar's heart the road on which he was to travel. The call was really nothing more nor less than obedience to the Will of God from now on. "It was up to me to follow Him in faith and obedience," he said later.

The first two years as a medical officer went by quickly as Kumar spent time establishing rapport with the field staff and the patients. The trips to the field clinics brought him into close contact with so much pain and suffering. He was being shown, at first hand, how the other half lived. Every face at the open-air clinics told a story of rejection, of fear, of brokenness and hopelessness. Leprosy patients with all kinds of deformities sat huddled together under the spreading trees, waiting for the clinic to start. Waiting for a sign of a miracle that would cure them. Waiting with hope. They had heard stories of Jesus reaching out and touching and curing people like them so many years ago. Now, they waited for his disciples to reach out and touch them too and cure them.

Kumar was always aware of his calling to be a missionary. There was no glamour attached to it. Just plain hard work, a constant giving and emptying of himself. With his first salary, he bought himself a reference Bible with a concordance. Spending time reading the Bible and soaking himself in God's Word and in prayer became priority for him. He was naturally blessed with a caring, generous heart. Now seeing so much suffering around him, his sensitive heart opened out even more.

The patients adored this young man who always had a kind word for them and treated them as real human beings. There was Munuswamy, a seven-year-old, whose fingers had just begun to claw. His father had abandoned the family when Munuswamy was a baby and he was raised by his mother who was a very sickly woman. Little Munuswamy was a shepherd boy and looked after several families' sheep and goats. He was paid a pittance for this and it was with this small amount that he and his mother lived.

Kumar's heart went out to the little boy. He put his arms around Munuswamy's thin shoulders and drew him close. "Come with me to Karigiri hospital. The doctor there will operate on your fingers and make them straight, just like mine. Then, we can teach you to do something better than looking after other people's sheep. You can even go to school if you like. There is no need for you to hide away from the others. What do you say Munuswamy, will you come with me?"

Seeing the boy's eyes light up with hope, Kumar went across the village to Munusamy's house to see his mother. He was shocked to see a small mud hut with a tattered thatched covering. It was monsoon time and the clouds were darkening and rumbling, threatening rain. When he left the house, Kumar emptied out his purse to the paramedical worker in that village and said, "Can you get this roof fixed by this evening? If you need to pay any extra to get it done quickly, say so and I will send you some more."

Munusamy and his mother were not bothered by the rainy season that year for the first time in their lives.

A disease like leprosy is no respecter of a person's wealth or status. There were wealthy landlords too who had leprosy. To them the burden of this disease was even worse. Ashamed of their deformities, they rarely ventured out and lived a lonely life within their own homes. Kumar visited these isolated rich families and was welcomed with great joy. He took with him his humour and his own brand of caring and warmth. He sat on the floor with them and shared their meal, relishing the simple food, complimenting the women in the family on the cooking, playing with the children, looking at the books of the school-going youngsters. Such visits always brought hope and sunshine to these families. Many were afraid to leave their homes for surgery. Kumar's assurances and faith often helped them to take a decisive step which, for many, would change their lives.

Now, standing outside the intensive care unit of this reputed hospital, so many of them were afraid that this man who had been a part of their lives for so many years would leave them forever, and they would have no one to turn to. No one who would care for them. No one who would touch them or love them. Most of the patients were Hindus, some were Muslim. At this moment, there were no barriers of religion. Their Creator was beyond all this. Their faith and prayers alone soared towards Him, asking for healing for Kumar.

Although my heart was so heavy, one thought flashed through my mind continually. "Thank You, Lord, that this happened at home and not on the journey to Vietnam or while in a strange country. Thank you for the memory of so many happy years."

Time passed slowly that night, as the monitor bleeped steadily and the electron beam drew its endless patterns on the screen. My mind swept back to the days when I had started out as a new bride.

4. Life In Karigiri

I could still remember the excitement and apprehension of leaving my parents' home to build a new one with Kumar. The road to Karigiri begins at the railway gate, off the main road between Madras and Bangalore. In the far distance, lies the hump-shaped hill, like a sleeping elephant. The road is long, straight and bumpy.

Kumar held my hand tight as the van took us to our new home. Huge trees, laden with finger-like brown tamarind pods, lined the roadside, providing a canopy of shade. The road cut through what looked like a forest. Splashes of bright-red and yellow dusted the tree tops. So many shades of green mingled into each other in the afternoon sunlight.

Kumar was excited at coming home. He explained that over forty years ago, Karigiri was a barren brown desert where nothing but a few thorn bushes grew. This desolate place, seventeen kilometres from the nearest town, was the only place available for a leprosy hospital. A sufficiently large area was just not available closer to the crowded town. And, in any case, people would not tolerate a leprosy hospital in their midst. The founders of this place realized that for Karigiri to survive as an institution, a new environment had to be created to make it more attractive for people to work and live there. So a unique experiment to forest this area began.

While explaining all this, Kumar pointed out various things to me. "Today, as you can see, Karigiri is a large campus in a lush green nature reserve."

It was a happy day for Kumar as he was bringing his bride home. For me, everything was new and a bit frightening. Sleep did not come easily that night. Eerie, throaty sounds kept waking me up. "It's only an owl," Kumar would say as he turned over and went back to sleep.

On my first morning, he woke me up saying, "We have a visitor."

Peter was the first leprosy patient I had ever seen. He stood before me, palms joined together in the traditional greeting. Except his hands were not really hands, for they had no fingers, just a thumb and knobbly stumps at the end of his palm. My eyes went down to his feet. My stomach tightened as I saw that he had no feet to speak of either. He balanced precariously on small heavy shoes that rolled as he walked. Peter brought out two garlands strung with yellow marigolds and white jasmines and hung them around our necks, welcoming us with a lovely smile.

Kumar accepted this graciously, and shocked me by putting his arm warmly around Peter. Carefully I moved away hoping that he wouldn't put the same arm around me. "This is my friend Peter. You'll be seeing a lot of him," he said.

After Peter had gone, I sat down on the grey stone steps of our verandah. Straight ahead of me, a huge rain tree sprawled its arms out in greeting to the morning sun. Perched on its branches, some black and white magpies watched me nervously. The early morning mist, the soft cooing of pigeons, and the fresh air, brought a sense of peace to my turbulent mind.

Kumar brought me a cup of steaming coffee and sat down beside me. "You are shocked at the sight of Peter aren't you, Ushamma? There are so many more just like him. These are not just my patients, some of them are also my friends. Peter, for example, used to come to my father for help when I was young. Now, he comes to me because he has no one else. All they need sometimes, is just someone to talk to them, care about them, laugh with them. You must never turn them away, or be rude to them, or make them feel that they are different from you. They have enough sadness in their lives and we should not add to it."

Nothing Kumar said earlier had prepared me for the kind of life I was to lead from then on. Over the months, I was introduced to Thangavelu, a charming old man who lived alone, as his family had thrown him out after it was discovered that he had leprosy. And Amara, a beautiful young woman from a wealthy family who was kept isolated because of her deformities. Pappa, who didn't have leprosy but another terrible skin disease, and young Munusamy to whom Kumar was a father figure. This motley crowd of people soon became my family and filled my life with their stories, their wisdom and their love.

Now eighteen years later, here they were, standing outside the intensive care unit in despair, praying for healing for their beloved doctor. Being with them all brought back so many vivid memories and reminded me of the days when Kumar was busy gathering data for his Ph.D. from the villages in Gudiyatham taluk. Then, on most days, he would leave on his motorbike around three or four in the morning so that he could catch up with his patients in their homes before they left for work in the fields. On other days, he would go to the village clinics and take me along with him. These were very special times for me. There, watching him at work, under the large leafy trees, seeing the way he related to people, I began to get a better understanding of him. His patience and humour were remarkable. So too were his compassion and his sensitivity.

The first time I saw Muniamma she was huddled inside a worn out grey blanket. Her complexion was dark brown, like parched earth, and deeply furrowed. A blob of a twisted, sunken nose gave her a clownish look. Her bony frame was wrapped in a dark blue sari. Sad, cloudy eyes gazed across at us with such a look of admiration and envy. I was surprised when Kumar told me that she was just my age, but looked so old because of the ravages of the disease. As she had no family, she lived on the verandah of the temple and lived on whatever food people gave her. She was one of his favourite patients and he brought her over to meet me.

'I like your wife, ayyah," she said, "She's very beautiful."

"I like her too," he said, "but I wish she had beautiful long hair like yours. I keep telling her to grow it but she won't listen to me."

Muniamma put her hands through her hair and smiled radiantly. She proudly twisted her long thick plait, decorated with bright orange flowers, to the front and showed it off to me. She went on to tell me, in great detail, how to oil my hair and wash it with gram powder to make it thick and luxuriant like hers. I realized that despite our very different backgrounds we were just two women at heart, discussing things women all over the world did with a natural ease.

Suddenly, her deformities did not matter and I began to see the woman beneath all the pain and suffering. Listening to her tale of rejection, of isolation and shame, my heart went out to her. Instinctively, I put my arm around her. It felt good to hold her and to see her smile shyly. She seemed so surprised and happy that I had touched her. She was the first person with leprosy whom I had touched, and looking at the joy in her face I now knew what touch meant to those whom society labelled as untouchable. I was grateful to Kumar for this experience and for teaching me how to reach out to someone in pain.

At every clinic, there were a few patients who would linger after all the others had gone. This was "togetherness time" with their doctor. No matter how long the clinic, they would wait, and provide sweet, tender coconuts for the whole team, or something spicy to eat.

At one clinic, the paramedical workers complained about a lady who would not take her treatment regularly. She just could not come to terms with the fact that she had leprosy and had tried to kill herself twice. Her deformities were very mild and not really noticeable. Yet, the stigma of leprosy, coupled with her own low sense of self-worth, was so harsh, that she just could not see any kind of a future for herself. Kumar explained to her that she could come to Karigiri where the social workers would help her choose a suitable programme of rehabilitation. She could learn to live again. "There is always hope. You never know, you may meet someone there and marry him. So many of our patients do so and live a happy life."

"Why would I want to live, sir? Who would marry someone like me?" she laughed, shaking her head.

It mattered not that the woman was twice his age, nor that all his staff were watching him, nor even that I stood by. Kumar gently put his arm around her thin shoulders and said, "You know, if I wasn't already married, I would marry you."

The woman doubled up with laughter and looked at him and smiled.

"What do you say, will you come to Karigiri and see the social worker?"

The woman nodded her assent. One more life had been touched by a kind gesture.

Our life at home followed a pattern of evening walks, regular Bible studies and dinner with friends. As the sun went down, the air cooled, and we would walk through the campus to the park and the pond. It was common to see families of fat little partridges also taking an evening stroll. High above us, fork-tailed swifts would chase each other happily, while the crows gathered noisily on the tree-tops. Now and then, a kingfisher would streak through the leaves, his turquoise wings a flash of colour amidst the green. These evening times with Kumar, in the midst of so much natural beauty, were moments of intense happiness for me, for he was always reassuring and proud of me for the way I was adapting to a new way of life.

During the day, I set about making a garden, planting all kinds of flowers in the front. Huge yellow sunflowers, delicate peach-coloured lilies, little pink roses and white daisies, all made a splash of riotous colour. At the back, I grew tomatoes and long green chillies to begin with. After I succeeded, I went on to french beans and all kinds of vegetables. Soon, we grew all our own vegetables.

Besides gardening, there was a whole menagerie of birds to look after. Kumar brought home a family of baby peacocks as a birthday present for me. To keep the peacocks company we had turkeys, guinea fowl and country hens. For a while, we even had a goat. I had become quite the farm girl.

I was also busy keeping an open home. People mattered more to Kumar than anything else. From the beginning, our home was open to the many foreigners who passed through Karigiri on various training programmes, to all his staff and to his patients. Kumar's charm was magical and a balm to anyone who was lonely or afraid.

Often, I too was lonely, away from my parents in England and all that I was used to. I had been independent for a while, had earned a good salary, had worn beautifully co-ordinated clothes, and now none of that mattered. Kumar's salary of seven hundred rupees vanished even before he brought it home, as there was always someone who got to him first with some pressing need. Besides this, there were two people that he was putting through school and college. Sometimes, I was so exasperated by his generosity that I would cry in frustration, "There's no money left, what are we going to live on for the rest of the month?"

"Don't fuss darling, we'll go over to my mother's. She'll be thrilled to have us over for a few days," he would reply.

On Saturday evenings, the families in Karigiri would take the hospital bus to Vellore, seventeen kilometres away, to do our shopping. This was the highlight of my week—my outing to the local market! We would take our time buying the few vegetables and provisions we needed and would meet up with some of Kumar's friends for a while. I would look forward to this trip the whole week, but once we actually got on the bus, I would begin to dread it.

Vellore was a noisy congested town with no pavements or a drainage system. So, one had to walk on the road vying for space with the cows, the bicycles, the buses and all the other people. The market in the evenings was dimly lit, crowded and alive with sound. The vendors yelled out the names of vegetables and fruits in a loud sing-song voice and called out if they recognized us. The sight of all the vegetables, neatly piled into pyramids, always fascinated me. So did the many pungent smells. Here too, one jostled with goats and cows, while balancing shopping bags.

One day, while returning to our bus, we saw a tattily dressed English woman sitting by the roadside. Beside her stood an equally shabby man, his long hair in disarray. They seemed to be having some kind of argument and the girl was crying.

""You go ahead," said Kumar, "I'll catch up with you."

When he returned, he had the couple with him. "Ushamma, this is Tom and Jane. Jane is not very well, so they will be staying with us for a couple of days."

I glared at him. Was he out of his mind? We didn't know these people and heaven knew what kind of germs they were carrying for it looked as if they hadn't washed for days. Kumar chatted to them pleasantly all through the journey, making up for my ill-humour.

Alone in the privacy of our room, I fell on my bed and sobbed. "You can't do this to me. What if they rob us in the middle of the night or murder us?"

Kumar just laughed. "Believe me, they haven't the energy for either. Actually, Ushamma, she's quite sick. She's just miscarried."

"Are they married?"

"I don't think so. Anyway, it's not up to us to judge them. At the moment, they just need rest, a place to stay, and good food."

"Why couldn't she go to a hospital?"

In reply to this, Kumar handed me his Bible. It was open at the story of the Good Samaritan. "Tell me, Ushamma, if you were in a strange land and you were sick, wouldn't you want someone to help you?" End of conversation.

I hung my head in shame and despair. Will I ever match up to his goodness, I wondered. So many people had been touched by his kindness and thoughtfulness... ...Now, years later, I saw each message of goodwill and wishes for his recovery as a tribute not only to his generous heart, but also to the way he lived.

Watching him lie there so pale and still, I couldn't believe that this was happening to us. The slow rhythmic rise and fall of his chest, an occasional groan, or a kick of his arm or leg, told me that this was no dream but brutal reality. To focus my thoughts on something positive, I kept thanking God for all the good days of our life together. So many people I knew had rough marriages and were breaking up. We had been blessed with such good memories.

Throughout our years together, we had both learnt several lessons in nourishing our marriage. The giving of gifts was very important to both of us as it showed, in tangible ways, that we loved and cared for each other.

Kumar used to buy a length of fragrant white jasmine for me to wear in my hair every day. On our first wedding anniversary, there was a big parcel sitting on my bed as soon as I woke up. Excitedly, I opened it to find it was a vessel with which to make idlis.

"How could you give me such a terrible thing as an anniversary present?" I cried.

"I thought we needed one. You were always saying you wanted one."

"Yes we need one, but in no way is it a personal affirmation of your love for me."

He took me in his arms and was most apologetic. We both learned that nourishing each other did not mean giving each other what we thought the other person needed, but what the other person wanted. We learned to understand each other's needs and desires and to cherish and nourish our love in ways that were pleasing to each other.

One afternoon he came home with a surprise present for me. A recording of the Beatles.

"Not quite your style is it?" I commented.

"No, but I knew you'd like it."

My heart warmed to him.

The memory of that warmth now flowed into me as I sat in the bleak, comfortless cold of the intensive care unit. Little snapshots of our life together kept drifting in and out of my mind as I sat beside Kumar. I smiled at the memory of that first anniversary. There had been seventeen more since then, and Kumar had taken care to make each one of them romantic and special. Were we not to have any more? Reality hit me once again as I saw Kumar lying there so pale and lost among the maze of tubes that went in and out of him. Occasionally, there was a groan, a shriek of pain and I plunged again into despair. The thought of tomorrow, another long day of uncertainty, made me numb with fear.

To escape the cloying atmosphere of the ICU, I went outside. From the balcony where I stood, I could see through the white arch of the chapel. The lights inside were soft and prayers were being said. I stood there for a while, lost in my own thoughts until the familiar words of the hymn woke me up.

"The darkness deepens; Lord with me abide;

When other comforts fail and helpers flee,

Help of the helpless, Lord abide with me."

I was surprised to see so many of Kumar's paramedical workers come out of the chapel. "We have been here all evening," they said. Many of them had tears in their eyes. "Don't worry, sister, God will surely hear all our prayers." They produced little notes of hastily scrawled Bible promises, and verses on scraps of paper, to help me keep faith. Someone handed me a cup of strong, hot coffee and a plate of chappathis. The faith of these men and their love for Kumar moved me deeply. I should not have been surprised for I knew that the ties that bound them went back a long way to when Kumar was a raw young doctor.

During his early days in the department, he had travelled with them on foot, and on bicycle, on their village routes. After work, he visited their homes and got to know their families. He also understood their problems. The men would leave while it was still dark, after a breakfast of the previous night's cold rice and some pickle, carrying a packed lunch for later. At nights, they would return to their homes exhausted, and find themselves confronted by leaking houses or wives and children who needed something for which money was scarce. To Kumar, the problem of the men's exhaustion was easily remediable. He suggested to the Director at Karigiri that the paramedical workers be given motorbikes. This recommendation, made at a time when motorcycles for private or official use was seen as a status symbol, did not endear him in any way to the administration, but it wove a bond between his staff and himself for the sympathetic concern that he evinced towards them.

Govindan was a smear technician in Karigiri, whose mother, a widow, sold vegetables on the roadside. Although he came from a very poor famiiy, he had lofty dreams that he often shared with Kumar. He was also one who frequently got into trouble and therefore not much liked by everyone. Kumar understood his frustration and felt sorry for him. To help him, he put aside part of his salary every month so that he could pay for Govindan to finish his school exams, even as he continued working. Once this was successfully done, he encouraged and paid for him to do a bachelor's degree course by correspondence, while still working at the lab in Karigiri. After this, seeing Govindan's aptitude and his desire for social work, he paid for him to do a master's degree in social work.

It was difficult for someone with Govindan's background to get admission into the Madras School of Social Work. Kumar went personally to see the Director and persuaded him to give Govindan a chance. Two years later, Govindan graduated with distinction and his dream of being a social worker was fulfilled.

Now, Govindan stood before me, weeping. "What will happen to us, sister?" he cried.

"Don't cry for him, pray for him instead," I urged them all. I could understand their pain and their fears. For if Kumar did not wake up, they stood to lose not just a good boss, but a loving friend, a father figure and a benefactor as well.

One of them showed me his watch. "See ma'am, Dr Kumar gave this to me." About a dozen of them showed me their watches. Kumar had given them all a watch similar to the one he normally wore. I smiled when I remembered how this came about.

After his return from London, one of the field staff admired Kumar's watch which was a present from my Dad. It was beautiful. "Where sir, can we ever afford one like this?" he said. Kumar promised him that on his next trip abroad, he would get him a similar one, and keep his promise he did. Soon, all his staff wanted a watch and he promised them all one sometime before either he, or they, retired. Thus a watch for one or more of his staff became a regular part of Kumar's shopping list on his successive trips abroad.

His generosity was part of his charm. Often, it was misunderstood as a kind of arrogance. Kumar believed that all that he had came from God, and whenever an opportunity offered itself, it gave him great pleasure to share things with others. Many of those whom his generosity had touched were here beside me now.

In spite of being surrounded by so many caring people, I felt so alone and afraid. It had become a habit with me, whenever I was paralyzed by fear, to think of something good, to count my blessings. But now, standing there in the cold night, my mind just went blank. To help me concentrate, I brought my hands together and clasped them in an attitude of prayer. Bright gleams from my ring caught my eye, reminding me of another time when the same ring brought so much joy, but was also a harbinger of what was unfolding now.

5. The Dreadful Secret

A flash of sparkle gleamed across my half-open eye. A warm feeling of joy spread through me as I swung my hand close to my face. Nestling there on my finger was a large glittering diamond, the biggest I'd ever seen or worn.

"With all my love, now and forever, in this world and the next." With these words and a kiss, this ring had been slipped onto my finger the night before by the man snuggling deep into my shoulder.

Holding him in my arms, watching the easy rise and fall of his chest, I was wide awake and thankful for his safe return. It was a fresh new morning bursting with all kinds of promises. Kumar was still asleep. I slipped out of bed and hugged the memories of the night to myself.

After a while, feeling bored, I looked through all the travel magazines he'd brought back and tried to imagine the places he had been to. Hoping to find more, I opened his briefcase. As I ruffled through the papers, I came across my name.... "My darling Ushamma," Smiling to myself, I picked up the letter which hadn't been posted and settled down with a cup of coffee to read it.

Kumar's letters were usually wonderfully romantic and after three months of being on my own, I was ready for the kind of loving that only a passionate husband could give. But my hands shook and my eyes blurred as I read on, for these were not the words I expected to see.

"How do I say the things that I want to say to you? I love you, I need you so badly and you are so far away... our life together is going to fall apart... this dreadful disease has taken over and I am so afraid.... how terrible for you to be a widow at forty and to raise the boys alone.... The end, when it comes, will be a horrible one.... I will end up vomiting blood and going into a final coma. Please help me face it bravely . . ..It will be a terrible time for you, I'm so afraid for all of us. I wish you were here with me.... please don't leave me .... please don't stop loving me.... I have no one but you, I know this is too much to ask of you...."

I read the letter again and again and each time my stomach wound tighter and tighter. Immersed in my thoughts, it was sometime before I realized that Kumar had joined me outside. There was no trace of worry or fear on his face and I wondered if I had imagined it all. He seemed cheerful and fresh after his bath.

"Did you sleep well?" I asked.

"The first night of sleep for three months," he smiled and pulled me into his arms. Expecting lots of kisses, he was stunned by my sobbing.

"What's wrong? What's the matter?"

I opened my hands and there crushed and tear-stained lay the letter.

"Oh no! I wish you hadn't seen that. I wrote it at a time when I was really low, but decided not to post it to you. I didn't want to upset you just now."

"Is it true?" I asked, hoping he would say no.

He slowly nodded his head and clutched me closer.

"How could this be? What is this killer disease and where did you get it from? How long have you known about it? Why didn't you tell me?" I threw so many questions at him, afraid of the answers.

"As a medical student, I used to donate blood whenever any one needed it. Each time, the blood was used only after testing negative for hepatitis B. But the eighteenth time I donated blood turned out to be the last time my blood was used. Three months later, when I gave blood again, it was rejected, as I was found to be positive for hepatitis B. Most likely, the needle used the previous time to draw blood had been contaminated with the hepatitis virus. It didn't affect me in any way at the time and I hoped that it would resolve itself. Usually, these things do and I just assumed that it was all over. I had forgotten all about it until l went for that last check up three months ago just before I went to Papua New Guinea. Quite accidentally, the doctor who examined me found that my liver and spleen had become enlarged and liver function tests showed that the enzyme levels were way beyond normal. What l have now is chronic active hepatitis B. In a few years it will develop into cirrhosis of the liver and that will be the end."

"How could you have kept it from me all these days? You poor darling." I gathered him into my arms.

"l'm sorry, I just didn't want to hurt you. I didn't know how you would react. I was so scared and alone in Papua New Guinea, brooding over this horrible secret. Every night, I would return to that empty hotel room and think of what the future holds for us and I couldn't bear it. I felt so alone."

Kumar had unburdened himself by writing a letter to me, but with no intention of actually letting me see it. Thus he could give full vent to his feelings. What he did intend to give me was the diamond ring costing a good part of his earnings on this assignment. But now that I had chanced upon this painful secret, I could see the relief that someone else knew flood his face. We held each other for a long time and cried. Horrible and undesired as this revelation was, its decisive significance would emerge only later. But it started us off on a pattern of mutual self-disclosure and sharing whatever was on our minds, which was to prove crucial much later.

For Kumar, the fact that he had a life span of only about five years, was really hard to come to terms with. For me, all this was terrifying and yet, as I looked at my poor shaken husband, I knew that I would somehow have to be the source of strength he so badly needed. There were so many worries on his mind.

"Should I look for a job that will pay more? We need to save as much as we can in the next few years, otherwise what will happen to you? Should we tell your parents? What about our children?"

The worries were beginning to hit me too. What would I do if something happened to him? I would have no job, nowhere to live, and two small children to raise on my own. Panic began to surface through me too. I caught the look of immense sadness in his face as huge tears rolled down again. In all our years together, I had never seen such grief or confusion in him and it pierced my heart.

"Money will be our last priority," I said, quite certain that what I was saying was the right thing to say. "What should matter is being together and being as happy as we can under the circumstances, for as long as we can. From now on, we will do everything you have always wanted to do. Travel whenever you can. Do as much work and research as you can. Be together as much as we can. We will still carry on as normal a life as possible, knowing that time isn't on our side. One more thing, no more secrets from each other please, let's share everything, however painful it may be. And let's not worry about what anyone else will say. This is our life, and hereafter we will live it the way we want to and in the way that will make sense to us."

I slid to my knees in front of him, and cradling his beautiful face in my hands, prayed with all my heart for healing. Our children were so young. Jamie was looking forward to his seventh birthday and John-John was just four. Please Lord, hear our prayer, heal Kumar and restore him to good health to serve you as he has always done.

6. Our Days In Singapore

Our whole way of life changed from this point. There was an intensity and passion to everything that Kumar did. In 1991, there was a request from The Leprosy Mission in London asking if Kumar would be interested in setting up an Evaluation Unit for the Mission in Singapore. It was an assignment for two years, after which Kumar could return to Karigiri.

For a while now Kumar had been praying, asking God, "What do you want me to do?" His calling had been to work in the field of leprosy in Karigiri. But at work, not everyone shared his passion or his views. Often, he was at odds with the administration for championing the underdog, for demanding justice for a co-worker or for securing better working conditions for his staff. Relationships between the Director of Karigiri and Kumar were unusually strained and Kumar often wondered how he could possibly continue working there without compromising on his calling. He felt that unless God gave him clear instructions, he would remain where he was, regardless of all the problems that came his way.

The timing of the offer from The Leprosy Mission was right, the Director at Karigiri was more than happy to have Kumar off his hands, and for us it seemed that God was leading Kumar to something new within the framework of his earlier calling. We moved to Singapore in July 1991.

Kumar's days in Singapore were filled with travelling. His diabetes was under control, but there were other concerns as a liver biopsy revealed that there were signs of cirrhosis of the liver. For much of the time, he was in excruciating pain, his feet were swollen and he was on a lot of medication, but he was not going to let anything deter him from his work. He felt that each assignment he had was specially given to him by God and certainly it seemed that God often took him to strange exotic places where few people from India had ever been.

In Ethiopia, he stayed in a shack of a room with no toilet facilities. Hearing that the toilet was in the yard outside, he opened the door one night to find a young man with an AK47 machine gun outside his door. "We shoot anything that moves in the night, sir, so please don't come out."

During a conversation with the young soldier he learned that many boys like him were dragged away from their homes by the army and most never went back. Thousands of young lads were maimed and sat around in camps waiting for treatment. This young soldier was lucky, as he had settled in quickly to army life, and had not been abused much. But he hadn't seen his family for over five years. Spending time with such unusual people, listening to them, befriending them and sometimes treating them medically, became part of his travelling mission too.

In South Africa, he was responsible for evaluating the many leprosy programmes within the Mission and on his advice many changes were made.

Travelling to West Africa, in Nigeria, Guinea Bissau and Conakry, he was invited by the governments and the World Health Organisation to evaluate their programmes there. At one centre, the Dutch Director remarked, "I never thought I would live to see the day when an Indian would come to evaluate the work of white men in Africa."

To missionaries working in these far off places, Kumar's presence was inspiring and refreshing. He brought them news from within the Mission, listened to their problems and frustrations. He often played the role of mediator in difficult relationships. He was also a bit like Father Christmas. ... he presented the newest videos, perfumes, tapes of music, and tinned food as gifts to those who worked in these isolated places. And they loved him for it.

Assignments for the WHO took Kumar to the island of Tonga, the Solomon Islands, Vanuatu, the Mariana Islands, Cook Islands, Fiji, Guam, Marshall Islands, Indonesia and the Philippines. His work entailed making honest evaluations of existing programmes and then making recommendations that were both practical and suitable to that region, and finally, making sure that these were implemented.

He loved the travelling, the new places and experiences. He sampled local delicacies like raw fish, snake, turtle and every possible kind of meat. He swam in the Pacific until sharks chased him out of the water. He went fishing with local fishermen for tuna and marlin, went snorkelling and scuba diving in coral-laden seas and dived in crystal clear water, looking for oysters to bring pearls for me.

Most of the assignments lasted a period of three months, and Kumar had ample time to make good friends. He eagerly sought out Indian families to lessen his homesickness. Wherever he went, the local church was always his main support and point of fellowship. He joined Bible study groups, led discussions and built solid relationships wherever he went. Often, he played the role of counsellor for marriages and families in trouble. He carried with him pictures of his family, his patients and little drawings and letters from the children which he pasted onto the wall of his room to relieve his homesickness.

Many times, he brought back little gifts for me from families to whom his presence brought peace and comfort. The messages that accompanied these gifts were almost always the same. "Having him with us was like a breath of fresh air." Often he said that it seemed as if God had taken him to that particular place not just for leprosy work alone but to bring peace and love to some family in need of healing. He brought healing and comfort wherever he went.

On one such trip, he found a beautiful young Indian girl, almost a slave to her husband and badly physically abused. She had no money and lived a miserable life. Talking to the husband did not help. The girl was sick and almost suicidal. As he was leaving, Kumar gave her a sheaf of bank notes saying, "If you ever need to buy yourself a ticket home to your family, use it."

Travelling also brought its share of adventure. In Zaire, a young man promised him extra money for his American dollars. The man took him into a shop, gave him the notes, and asked him to count them very carefully. While Kumar was busy counting, the man disappeared. Much to his dismay, he found that the first note and the last note were real, the rest in between were newspaper cut-outs.

As these assignments were for a long period of time, being alone without a family was not easy, and he had his share of unseen struggles. Often the places he went to were abundant in attractive women who were more than willing to spend time with a handsome generous man. Some were extremely intelligent and articulate colleagues of whom he was very fond. In Manila, at a reception held for him at a local judge's residence, his hostess was shocked that he had been alone for nearly two months. "Let me find you a nice girl, who won't cause you any trouble when you have to go back," she said. When Kumar protested, she said, ""Don't be shy, everybody does this nowadays," and produced a beautiful girl before him.

"You have no idea how hard it was for me to say 'no' to her, Ushamma," he told me later. "I only got through the rest of the evening by thinking of all the good things we share together and by remembering what it is like each time I come into your arms, feeling clean, honest and faithful within myself."

His return home was always a cause for celebration. The children would decorate the house with fresh flowers, streamers, coloured lights and huge 'welcome home' messages. Few people could understand the excitement and relief that his return meant for us as a family. All the while he was away, the children and I would pray, "Lord please keep him with you, keep him in good health and bring him back safe to us."

Our families and friends were sometimes very angry with me for allowing or encouraging Kumar on his travels. "He should stay home and rest ... what if something should happen to him on his travels?" It was hard to explain that we had committed ourselves to living as full a life as possible under the circumstances and we had asked God to take care of him while he was away from us. The boys would pray for him every night, sometimes tearfully, as they missed him so much. John-John, as a small boy, would wait at the airport with such an anxious look on his face until he spotted Kumar. Then he would clap his hands and jump up and down with joy. No matter how late he got home, Kumar would unpack his suitcases and bring out wonderful gifts, rich silk from Thailand, coral from Fiji, pearls from the islands and in a few days, he would be off again.

When his assignment in Singapore was nearly over, Kumar was offered a permanent position with the Mission and we had to decide whether to return to Karigiri or stay on in Singapore. Both our families and close friends advised us to stay on. Life in Singapore was so easy, it was a well paid job, we had a beautiful home and we belonged to a wonderful caring church. Both of us were part of a Bible study group which strengthened our faith and taught us how to live caringly in a community. I was a journalist with *The Straits Times* and had many interesting assignments. The boys were at a good school which encouraged their talents—James in athletics and art, and John-john in craft and writing. The family was happy and well settled. But Kumar had a commitment to Karigiri which few could understand. We prayed for guidance to stay or return.

To return meant coming back to the old setup of frustration and harassment at Karigiri. It also meant coming back with open hearts and discarding all the anger and bitterness of the past years. It meant accepting the present administration and not fighting it or trying to find fault with it. It meant letting go of old relationships and memories which brought us both much pain. Here in Singapore, we were free of the tension and pain caused by difficult relationships. To everybody else, it seemed such an easy decision to make. We could not understand why it was so hard for us. We prayed again and again for guidance. Once more Kumar felt his calling strongly. The message from God was, "Trust me, and I will take care of you." So we returned to Karigiri in 1993.

Healthwise, Kumar's liver was at a stage where doctors felt that treatment with interferon might help. A check up just before we left Singapore showed that Kumar had sero-converted from positive to negative and interferon, which was very expensive, was therefore not needed. His health in general seemed to be stable, though the pain and sleeplessness bothered him continuously. The fighting part of his nature was determined not to give in to this disease. When in pain, he would often just take a pain reliever and carry on working. To have given in to the pain, and taken time off for it, was seen as a sign of weakness and sickness, so he put on a brave face for everyone. Especially for the children, James and John.

Often, he would take them on long walks in the evening no matter how tired he was or despite the pain, his gun on his shoulder, and they would return joyously with partridges or rabbits for me to cook. Sunday mornings were often spent fishing or climbing Karigiri hill, not only with our children but with a handful of campus kids.

Now sitting beside Kumar in the ICU, my memories of Singapore seemed so close and fresh. And as I recalled the ways in which Kumar developed a loving relationship with the boys, realized that I had not given much thought to the confusion Kumar's coma would have caused Jamie and John-John.

The thought of the children reminded me that I had one rather sad task to perform. I went home from the hospital to explain to the boys that their father was seriously ill. From the time Kumar's illness was first diagnosed in 1989, we had been honest and shared everything with the children. We had decided against a cover up which would perhaps protect them for a while, but would then erect a barrier between us eventually. Time was so precious to us and living well, sharing, caring and being open and aware of each other's feelings were far more important than pretending that everything was alright. It was also a way of giving the boys the chance to decide for themselves how to react. They knew that their father had this disease which often made him very tired and ill. They knew that he was often in great pain. They knew too that they wouldn't have him with them for a long time. Both Jamie, who was seven at the time, and John-John, who was almost four, chose to go through the pain of being close to their father and loving him, rather than staying away cocooned in childishness.

Thus as they grew up, they became very supportive of him, they took care of him with great tenderness and were very gentle with him when he was in pain. The boys would often sit beside him stroking his forehead or kissing his stomach during terrible times of pain. They knew too that their father's health could worsen at any time, so being with him was always priority for them.

Now they were heart-broken, especially John-John. There were no words to comfort this weeping child, so I just held him close to me and cried with him. Hope, I realized, is a vital necessity of life, and we clung to that. I prayed for strength for us all and for a sense of hope through the anguish and helplessness of the situation we were in. This was monsoon season and there was a steady drizzle outside. Everything was damp and grey. Inside us, it felt the same. Jamie made a tape for his father so that I could play it for him, hoping that the sound of his voice would bring Kumar back into consciousness. Through his tears he spoke into the tape recorder, "Hello, Appa, I love you. I miss you. Please wake up soon. It's raining outside, Appa, it's dark and all the birds are going home to sleep. I'm thinking of you all the time, Appa, and praying for you. I love you, Appa."

7. An Unexpected Gift

Back at the hospital, it was a long wait. My mind went back to the many times I had sat and waited beside Kumar in hospital at other times. He had a tendency to produce stones in his bladder, which required surgery. As the disease progressed, there were several occasions when he was admitted for internal examinations, each of which left him exhausted with pain and anxiety.

Towards the end of 1995, a check-up had revealed that varices, a distension of normally invisible blood vessels, had developed where the food pipe (oesophagus) opens into the stomach. Left unattended, these bulging veins would eventually burst, and cause severe bleeding. These varices were already responsible for two mild bleeds which caused us great anxiety. It was recommended that they be "banded" or sclerosed to forestall further bleeding. This was a lengthy, painful procedure. Every week, for six weeks, Kumar had to go into hospital for three days. Each time, a large flexible tube called an introducer was slid down his throat. Through it would be passed a gastroscope, a long flexible rod about one centimetre thick, carrying the gadget for observing and treating the varices. As only one varice could be treated with each passage of the scope, the rod had to pass in and out a number of times during each session.

Kumar used to dread these sessions as no anaesthetic was given and the whole procedure was so agonizing. He used to shrink from the pain, but each time, God, in his love for Kumar, provided a kind and gentle person to sit with him, to hold his hand and talk to him gently throughout the operation, to provide such relief as was possible. For the first few times it was Dr George Kurian, Kumar's friend, a gastroenterologist. On occasions when George was out of town, other young doctors, who were part of the gastroenterology team, understood Kumar's fears and offered to sit with him and hold his hand. The kindness, compassion and gentleness shown by these doctors made us both deeply grateful for so much care. At times when we felt burdened by the pain and the general disruptions these admissions brought to our family life, such acts of kindness strengthened us. They helped us believe that even through these difficult times, God our Father also sent good things and blessings our way.

During this very traumatic time, something rather unexpected and wonderful happened to us. On a chance visit to an orphanage with a friend one day, I came across a little baby girl. So tiny, so fragile, so perfect. I picked her up and held her to me for a while. The warmth from my body must have seeped through to her, for she snuggled deeper and made herself very comfortable against me. Her fingers were like match-sticks covered with skin. But they clung to my fingers with a strong grip. I realized this baby was special to God, just as all babies are, and yet, for some reason, she was here alone. I wondered about what His plan was for her life, tucked away here in this lonely place. There seemed to be so much suffering in our world. My heart went out to her and I felt as weepy and as vulnerable as I did when each of our two sons were placed in my arms for the first time. I knew with some strange certainty that this baby was somehow going to be woven into the fabric of our life. I seriously thought of adopting her. Kumar and I had talked about such a step in the past but had never done anything about it because of the hectic course of events after John's birth.

The nuns at the orphanage too were excited at the prospect of finding a home for the baby until they heard that we already had children of our own and that too boys. Afraid of possible discrimination against adopted daughters, they were very particular that their girls go only to families without children. But the young nun who laid the baby in my arms whispered to me as I left, "Madam, you pray for this baby. She needs someone to pray for her. If God wants her to be part of your family, all doors will open." It was an exciting thought.

Kumar and the boys too were happy with the idea. "Don't get your hopes up," my friend warned, "The nuns are very fussy about who they give their babies to."

That night I just couldn't sleep. There had been so much pain and worry in our lives recently, and I was sure that a new baby would bring joy and tenderness into our family. "Please God, wrap her up in the warmth of your love. Let her not be alone," I prayed.

Late that night, I had a call from the orphanage to say that if we were seriously interested, then we could think of adopting the baby. So far it had been easy. The idea of another child was exciting, but now Kumar had to see the baby too and I was a little apprehensive about this.

A daughter for Kumar had to be fair-skinned, black-haired and beautiful. This little baby was a little darker skinned than me, bald, had rashes all over her and was in no way beautiful to anyone but me. When the little bundle was put into his arms, she lifted her matchstick-like arms, reached out for Kumar's pocket and clung to it. I watched nervously as to what his reaction would be. He looked at her for quite a while, then he stroked her fingers and tickled her feet. She responded by smiling and gurgling. Bending down, he kissed her forehead and his tears splashed like raindrops onto her tiny cheeks, just like they did on to the cheeks of the boys when they were first placed in his arms. He was very reluctant to let go of her. When it was time to go, he prayed over her, "Thank you Father for this beautiful child and for giving her to us. Please keep her safe in your arms until we can take her home and keep her in ours."

We were excited and nervous at the thought of being parents again. The nuns called us at the hospital the next day and said, "You both seem to love the baby so much, why don't you take her home right now? We can deal with the legal side of it later." The children and I went to the shops and bought some pretty dresses, nappies and feeding bottles. The boys were equally excited as they chose her clothes.

Next morning Kumar was wheeled down to the endoscopy room to get his varices sclerosed. Waiting outside, I was aware of the terrible pain he was going through and prayed for healing for him. In spite of all the suffering, it was going to be a very special day for us, as we were going to bring the baby home and I felt God's presence with me so clearly that whole morning. It was my birthday that day, and it was as if warm caring arms were holding me close, reassuring me that this was His plan for us.

Kumar proudly carried his new daughter, dressed in a soft yellow dress, back to Karigiri. Needless to say, our families and friends were shocked. I was past forty, and Kumar was in and out of hospital every week. "What a thing to do at this stage of your life. How will you cope with the baby and Kumar?" they said.

Mallika (little jasmine flower), as we decided to call her, was constantly in Kumar's arms. Despite the pain in his throat, caused by the endoscopy, he would sing to her, rock her in his arms and put her to sleep. While she was in his arms, there was no pain. She became his "pain-killer." We had always wanted a daughter, but this was something we had never prayed for as we were happy with our boys. God, knowing our unspoken desires, blessed us with Mallika at just the right time, for she was the source of much joy and love in our family.

Those were days when we seemed to be surrounded by God's presence and His love. But now sitting beside Kumar, keeping watch as the hours dragged by, God seemed so far away. A sense of desperate loneliness was creeping all over me. I felt chilled right inside me and it seemed that nothing would warm me, not even these wonderful memories. So many people wanted to help but there was nothing anyone could do. I prayed again, "Please don't leave me alone. Give me your assurances that You are with me." Heaven seemed silent.

8. A Traumatic Awakening

It was three days since Kumar had gone into a coma. Towards the morning of the third day, he started to call my name. Then he opened his eyes and looked straight at me.

"Hello sweetheart, do you remember me?" I asked.

"Of course, you're my Ushamma."

Relief flooded through me as I realized that his memory was intact.

For Kumar, however, there was no joy, only terror at the awakening. The bright lights in the ICU dazzled his eyes. Tubes were passed down his throat and nose, there were multiple transfusion needles on his arms, and his feet were tied with restrainers. He tried to get up, but couldn't. He screamed in fright, "What's happening? What have you done to me? Why am I all tied up?"

I put my arms around him. "It's going to be okay, sweetheart, you've been very sick, but you're going to be okay now," I whispered.

"What happened?"

I knew that the sooner he knew the truth, the better he'd feel.

"You went into a coma, a coma caused by hepatic encephalopathy. You were unconscious for three days, and now you're out of it."

Disbelief spread all over his face. As he looked around the ICU he realized that it was true.

"I'm finished, I'm finished," he kept saying as tears rolled down his cheeks. My own heart was breaking, but at this point I needed to be strong for him. I dried my eyes and pushed through the maze of tubes that were between us and held him in my arms. He put his head on my shoulder and wept.

"It's not the end, sweetheart, God in His mercy brought you back to me again. We're together, I love you, we have some more time, that's all that matters. I'm so thankful to have you here with me," I whispered to him again and again. Kumar still wept uncontrollably. The ICU staff, who were experienced in fright and dislocation, reassured him gently and helped to calm him down.

After a while, he remembered the boys and wanted to see them right away. As soon as Kumar was awake, I called the boys to say that he was alright, and that his memory was intact, but that he was very weak. I had also warned them about the tubes and his fragile state so that they wouldn't be too shocked to see their father this way. When the boys arrived, they just clung to Kumar and wept. "Thank God you're alright, Appa," Jamie kept repeating, while stroking and kissing Kumar's forehead. John-John stood beside him on the other side and covered Kumar's hand with kisses and tears.

After three days of uncertainty and fear, the relief on their faces washed away all the tension and sadness. I stood back and observed what to me was a miracle. The nurses and the doctors on duty, who had seen such awakenings so many times before, were, for some reason moved by this one. Perhaps because of the very tangible love between Kumar and the boys. They came and stood beside me, sharing in our pain and our joy. There was not a dry eye in the room.

Part of the trauma of coming out of this kind of coma is the intense restlessness, the feeling of wanting to sit up and then to lie down again. The lights in the ICU, the constant high-pitched sound of bleeps on the monitors and the realization of all that had happened to him, upset Kumar a lot and made him even more restless and frightened. He was afraid to close his eyes in case he slipped into a coma again. He wondered if he had been there all alone for three days. I assured him that I had been beside him, holding his hand, talking to him all the time, since he went into the coma. Now that he was awake, I reassured him that I would not leave him.

I was so exhausted myself, both with tiredness and relief. Not having slept for three days and all the waiting was beginning to take its toll on me. My back was aching and my feet too were swollen with all the standing. Despite his own pain and confusion, Kumar was most concerned for me. There was the fear, too, of what this meant in the light of his liver disease.

Kumar was allowed to drink only sips of water and his tongue was parched. Around eleven o'clock at night, he was very thirsty and pleaded for a cold drink. The doctor on duty told me that I could give him a bottled drink like a cola. Where at this time of night could I get a cold drink? The ICU was on the second floor of the hospital and the nearest shops were a long way off. Seeing Kumar so restless and desperate, I picked up my bag and prayed,

"Father God, you know how tired I am right now and what I need, please help me. Please give me the energy and strength I need to walk to the shops and back."

As I walked out of the ICU into the darkness outside, I heard someone call, "Amma, amma." I turned around and was surprised to see my tailor.

"I've been waiting here since nine o'clock," he said. "I heard that Dr Kumar was admitted in hospital, and as I was locking up my shop tonight, something inside me said, go to amma, she needs you now. I came immediately but they wouldn't let me in. So I waited here all this time. I'm so happy to see you. Do you need anything, amma? Can I do anything to help you?"

I was so surprised to see him there and taken aback by what he said. Yes, there was something he could do to help me. I asked him to get me a couple of bottles of cold cola. As he scuttled off down the stairs, I saw that he was dressed in a white shirt and white dhothi. He looked like an angel to me. Despite my battered frame of mind, I knew that God had provided for me at that precise moment in the form of the man who sewed my blouses. Not through my family or my friends, but through a stranger almost, and a man of another faith. I had always believed in a God of love who cares and watches over His children, but now I knew that He even cared about my tiredness and my aching feet.

Overwhelmed by this act of grace and love, I stood outside the lCU for a while, facing the chapel. Since Kumar had woken up, I had held myself together and had appeared to be strong and in control of my feelings. It was cold and damp. I was so tired and frightened that I started to cry. A while later, a feeling of warmth enveloped me. My tiredness, the many fears and my tears, all just fell away from me. A gentle voice whispered in my heart, "I will provide for all your needs. Just trust in me." I could feel the graciousness of God's presence like a mist around me. The earlier feelings of pain and fear had melted away and I felt a strange peace in my heart. I knew then that we would have to face many harrowing crises and that our needs would be manifold in the days to come. God, in His mercy and loving kindness, had given me an example of how He knew exactly what I would need and how faithful He would be.

I had often heard it said that before times of great testing and pain, God reveals himself to us in a tender way so that we could hold on to Him, especially on days when He seemed far away. I was thankful for this experience, but also afraid of what it could mean.

Kumar was discharged from the ICU and put into a medical ward. He was very restless and weak. A lot of excess fluid had collected in his abdomen causing him terrible pain. Nothing could be done for the pain as all the pain relieving drugs would go through his liver and further damage it. So it just had to be borne. Nothing could be given for the restlessness either, as it could push him into another coma. He was put on a strict diet without protein and was allowed to eat only a thin sago porridge. He felt a terrible sense of loss that this could happen to him. "I wish I had listened to you more often and rested, Ushamma," he cried. Then he was angry with me, "Why didn't you take better care of me?"

I prayed again for strength and patience and love. He was going to need so much from me in the days to come. There was so much anger within him too, at the sudden twist of fate which had reduced him to this level. Sometimes the pain was so intense, Kumar just cried with it. Many friends came and prayed for healing, and for the removal of pain. One person said, "In everything, give thanks and praise the Lord."

"God is asking too much of me. Am I supposed to thank Him for all this pain?" he cried after our visitor left. "What kind of a God would allow so much suffering? I wish I had died."

I took his hands in mine and made him look at me. "I know the pain is terrible for you. I wish I could bear it for you. I wish I could take it away from you, but I can't. So we have to beat the pain by ourselves. I will massage you, give you a hot water bottle, do anything I can to ease the pain. What we shouldn't do is allow it to destroy us. I know there isn't any other way to deal with this. As with everything else, we will go through this together."

It hurt me so much to see him in pain and to be so helpless. He saw my tears and kissed them away gently. I laid my hands on his stomach and prayed for healing and an end to the pain. I sat cross-legged on the hospital bed, and cradled him in my arms like a baby. He closed his eyes and I began to rock him to sleep. "Sing for me," he said.

"The Lord's my shepherd, I'll not want,
He makes me down to lie,
In pastures green He leadeth me,
The quiet waters by."

He slept in my arms for three hours while I kept watch over him.

A few days later the nurse brought me a brown envelope. I opened it and found the bill from the hospital for the ICU treatment. The final total gave me such a shock. The bill was for twenty-five thousand rupees. Kumar was devastated. Although I was shocked, I wasn't as upset as he was, because I had been given a wonderful example of God providing for my needs. He had given me strength to look after Kumar day and night, had given me the wisdom to say the right thing at the right time, and so I knew that He would provide for all that we needed, including this bill. I shared with Kumar my experience with the tailor, hoping that he too would have the same faith and trust. The previous night was so bad, the pain relentless; and now added to it the worry of how to pay the bill. "Don't worry sweetheart, God will truly provide for all our needs," I said.

Kumar was angry with me now, "How can you tell me not to worry, just where is this money going to come from?"

I myself did not know, and I had no answers for him, but I knew that I had embarked on a journey of trust and faith and that there was no going back now.

Next morning, a cousin of mine visited and handed over a letter from my father in Madras. I put it aside to read later. We had so many visitors that day and Kumar had cheered up a little. Then remembering the letter, I opened it. "My darling child, my thoughts are with you. I know you will have a lot of expenses and all this will add

to your worry. I hope this will ease some of your burdens."
Enclosed was a cheque for twenty-five thousand rupees.

I held it out triumphantly for Kumar to see. "I told you
God would provide," I said. "And He did."

Kumar was still on a no-protein diet, no salt, no sugar
either, and he was really fed up. This was our twelfth
day in hospital and the strain of looking after him was
getting to me. I was tired and beginning to snap. "Stop
complaining about the food, we have so much to be
thankful for. We have each other and the children and
you're getting better," I said when he made a fuss over
his food.

This was the wrong thing to say to someone weighed
down by pain and the loss of so many freedoms. Kumar
turned away from me. A wave of loneliness and sadness
hit me. I didn't want to hurt him, I wanted so desperately
for him to get a little better, a little stronger so that I could
take him home. Yet I seemed harsh and impatient with
him at times. A prayer I had written down a while ago
came to mind,

"There have been times O Lord
When I have walked the hill tops with you'
When I have felt you near
And my heart has been warm
In the remembrance of blessings in the past.
But now
My heart seems cold and dry
Moods of depression come over me,
Prayer seems unreal.
You seem hidden.

Dark clouds come over me.
Descend to my spirit, let me hear you whisper
'Keep steady'
If you cannot give me warmth of feeling
Give me your desire for me,
Your hunger for me, your emptiness."

But even such lofty words could not heal the emptiness and despair within me at such times. I needed a practical sign that God still cared and was with us.

Dr Zachariah, a former professor of Kumar's, and his wife Anna, were close friends of ours. They had been beside me during these days in hospital, sharing my worries and fears, and were a source of strength for me. Just when I needed a positive sign from God, Uncle Zac walked in. He could sense the aloofness between us and looked concerned.

"Kumar, I'm going to take care of you for a while'" he said and arranged his pillows into a more comfortable position for him. At that moment, lunch arrived. My heart sank. I knew how much Kumar hated the food and was in no mood for another battle.

"I'm going to feed you," said Uncle Zac. He picked up the spoon and began to feed Kumar, talking to him gently all the while, until everything was finished. I sat back and watched this display of love with tears in my eyes.

To any one who asks, does God really care, does He care about the little details of our lives, I would answer an emphatic "yes." That day too, I had seen Him not only care, but provide also, in the form of a loving friend, when I was feeling worn out and shattered. He showed me again that He gives us not only what we need when we need it, but that He gives us the best when we least expect it.

Kumar's doctors, Dr George Kurian and Dr Anand Zachariah, were always reassuring and wanted us to think positively about reorganizing our lives before we went home. Patterns of sleep, diet, exercise and work had to be changed. Once the period of rest was over, Kumar could go back to work. He could no longer travel alone, but they saw no reason why he could not carry on with his work in Karigiri.

This gave us some hope for it meant that we could still have a normal life. We spent a lot of time talking to each other about all that had happened, and what it was supposed to mean to us. Our readings from the Bible that week were all about change, about leaving all that is familiar and starting out afresh, trusting only in God. We were certain that God was showing us a new way to live. To slow down, to concentrate on what really mattered. To re-establish warmth and love into all our relationships.

9. Tears, Turmoil And Glimpses Of Joy

Once we were home, the period of rest and rehabilitation began. We placed a bed for Kumar out on our verandah overlooking the garden and spent most of the morning there. The marigolds and other yellow flowers were all in bloom and the garden looked fresh and lovely. Many patients and staff of Karigiri came to visit Kumar and it was good to be surrounded by so much love.

Mallika was thrilled to have us home again and spent her time playing beside us. She was now a year old, could walk and say "Appa." Every now and then she would scramble on to the bed, put her arms around Kumar and give him plenty of sloppy kisses. Kumar's feet were badly swollen with excess fluid, so he had to have them raised most of the time. Mallika would lift his feet and place them gently on a pillow. We used to massage his feet with oil to prevent them from becoming dry and cracked. Soon this became her job too. I marvelled at the sensitivity and tenderness of a one-year old. While she was with Kumar, he felt no pain. She made him laugh at her babyish antics. When she was beside him, there was always the incentive to get well, to provide for her, to be there for her as she grew up.

This was also a period when we spent a lot of time earnestly seeking God's Will in our lives. Reading the Bible and spending time in prayer had always been an integral part of Kumar's life. Now it became part of mine too.

For Kumar, his work, his international travel and reputation were so important. As a renowned epidemiologist, his advice and expertise were much sought after and he was a member of several policy making committees on leprosy, both in India and worldwide. The pilot studies he had done in Karigiri on multi-drug therapy for leprosy paved the way for the use of this drug regimen throughout the world. These and his earlier research work had resulted in a substantial body of publications in international scientific journals. As a teacher and trainer of leprosy personnel, he had spent several years producing excellent teaching material. As Deputy Director of Karigiri, he was involved in making plans for the future of the institution. He found it hard to accept that all this was now over so abruptly.

The period of rest at home was not an easy time for any of us. The doctors had advised strict bed-rest for Kumar. He found it hard to comply with this. I would find him wandering around the house looking for things to do. He had to be on a strict diet and this too upset him. Some of the time, I had to nag him about what the doctors advised and our relationship began to be strained.

School examinations were coming up for the boys and I had to make sure they did enough school work. They, however, preferred to spend their time sitting with their father, chatting to him or just being with him. They resented my nagging too.

To make things worse, the indignities of sickness were always present-pain, nausea, vomiting, weakness.

The pain would mangle him emotionally and spiritually and cut him off from me, which hurt and frightened me. Sometimes Kumar was so afraid of the dark and of going to sleep, in case he never woke up, that he forced himself to stay awake all through the night.

"Why, Why, Why," he would cry at times of great pain. "What have I done that I should suffer so?" By morning, he would be so weak and worn out that there was little joy at the thought of getting through another day. The pain often just drained us both, emptied us, divided us even and put a strain on other relationships too. There were times when I was snappy with the children when they made too much noise or when they demanded my time and attention with their problems. A friend, who called for the third time one day to enquire about Kumar, also got the bad end of my mood.

The final straw was when I saw two workmen painting a badminton court in our front yard.

"What's this?" I asked.

"They are putting in a badminton court for me. I want to play with the boys again and the court in the playground is too far for me to walk to," said Kumar.

"Are you crazy?" I screamed, "Don't you realize all those days are over. There's going to be no more days of badminton." Even as I finished speaking, I realized how cruel my words were. I did not have to look at Kumar's dejected face to see how much my outburst had hurt him.

"Why do I blow it so often, Lord?" I prayed, "Why do I hurt the one I love so much? Please grant me patience and love to keep going for all our sakes."

I had a book by Elisabeth Elliot, *A Path Through Suffering*, which spoke about suffering being either a wilderness in which we could be lost, or a pathway to God if we could accept it and release the outcome of it to God. This book ministered a lot to me and helped to answer a lot of my questions. I thought it may help Kumar too.

He got through the first few chapters and threw the book away in anger. "How can suffering ever be accepted? How can anyone who has not gone through physical pain write a book like this? I can never accept all this pain and suffering and thank God for it."

Who was I to say that in acceptance lies peace? I was not in his shoes. I was not crushed with pain. My life was not in ruins. The anger that the disease and the suffering had ignited within him, which had been suppressed all these days, now flared out into the open. Physical pain and emotional distress make terrible companions. There was no mystique in suffering, it was raw, ugly and relentless. It put a great strain between us.

"Grant me patience and large doses of love, help me to be gentle and loving always," became my constant prayer. About a year earlier, while reading the biography of the missionary, Lilias Trotter, I had been impressed with a phrase she had used while finding herself in situations of hardship. Now I remembered those words and this too became my prayer.

"Take the hardest thing in your life, the place of difficulty, outward or inward and expect God to triumph gloriously, right there in the very spot. Just there, He can bring your soul into blossom."

The hardest thing in my life right then was to be totally loving and calm all the time. Could God possibly bring my soul into blossom when most of the time I felt soulless?

Kumar and I were reading a biography of the missionary, Amy Carmichael, who worked in India and had started a home for children who would otherwise have become temple prostitutes. Amy suffered a broken leg, and for the last twenty years of her life was bedridden and in a lot of pain. She too had addressed many of the same questions that Kumar asked of God, and the book was beginning to influence us a lot.

"No earthly pain is forever,

Sorrow is lent

Joy is given.

Only the eternal lasts."

We began to understand that a thing that is lent can also be taken away at any time. A thing that is given is ours for keeping, for always. Only the eternal lasts. Both sorrow and joy are used for eternal purposes. Comfort like this often got us through a few hours. We debated on what eternal things were in our life at this moment. Kumar felt that friendship, love, the good memories and my devotion to him were eternal. I was touched to know what he felt about my devotion to him, particularly as I often felt stretched and tired, looking after everybody. I had very little time on my own. Even my time of solitude with God was getting less and less and this was beginning to tell on the way I too was beginning to look at life. Doubts were creeping into my mind. What if he never gets better? Should I look for a full-time job? Where was the God who assured me of never leaving me?

"The beginning of the end," that's how Kumar called this period. Sometimes, he was so depressed and wished he had died, then at other times he was so thankful to be with all of us again. There were so many worries too... What if the pain gets worse?.... How were we going to manage financially if there were no more assignments abroad?.... What would happen to him if his health got worse? .... Kumar was Deputy Director at Karigiri. Should he give up that post if he couldn't put in a whole day's work anymore?... Should he retire early, on medical grounds?.... Should we leave Karigiri and move to Madras and stay with my parents while Kumar did freelance work?

There were no easy answers to these questions. The doctors were unable to give us firm assurances or guidance. He had gone into coma so suddenly that it might not be a true indication of the final failure of Kumar's liver. With luck, he could continue without further such episodes for quite some time. Or he may have started on the first of a fatal series of comas at diminishing intervals. Only time and events would tell. We looked at all the options open to us and asked God to lead us through this difficult period of our lives.

Despite the pain and confusion, it was also a time of intense loving for the two of us. Holding each other, enjoying just being in each other's arms, our cheeks touching, of kissing and being kissed. This treasured time of intimacy and gentleness had only been possible because of the tragedy that had taken over our lives. It was also a time for sharing whatever was on our minds.

Kumar held my hands one day and said, "Sit down, I want to talk to you and I want you to listen to me. Please don't interrupt and please don't stop me." He was lying on his bed outside on the verandah. Mallika was playing beside us on the floor. I bent to pick her up and keep her in my arms.

"Leave her," he said and drew me into the warm circle of his arms."I want to talk to you about a possible end."

He saw my face stiffen and felt me move away. But he held me strongly and kept me against him. "We have to face it, Ushamma, I know it's upsetting, but we have to talk about it. I know that God has the power to heal me, I know that my waking up from the coma is quite a miracle. I know too that His Will will be done in my life, whatever that may be. And if His Will is to take me soon, then so be it, but I want to be prepared for it. I want you to be prepared for it as well."

I was shocked. Our life was getting into a pattern of normalcy, and all these fears had been pushed back from my mind. Now, Kumar was raking them all back into the painful forefront again.

"I want you to think about where you would want to go if something happens to me. I would be happy if you went back to live with Dad and Mum in Madras, but I realize that that may not be the best solution for you. If you want to stay on here in Karigiri, I'm sure the Director would give you a job in public relations. Or if you prefer to move to the town, we should start looking for a suitable place for you. I need to know your feelings too. You and the children are so young, I want you to rebuild your lives without me, to stay happy, to build a home again."

Holding me still in his arms, the tears started to flow, first mine, then his, till they all mingled together and soaked his shirt.

During times of great distress, I had learned that one simple way to find comfort is to choose the thoughts our mind can focus on—thoughts that are true, constructive and which bring hope. Otherwise false despair and self-pity could so easily eat into us. Now, I turned all my thoughts positively towards what Kumar wanted to discuss with me. I knew that Kumar was concerned for us as the head of our family, and that the plans and decisions that would have to be made in case things got worse needed to be discussed openly with him. He was giving me the chance to empty out all the worries and fears from my mind. I knew I had to do the same for him too, however agonizing it was going to be for both of us.

So we spent the afternoon discussing the merits of staying on in this area and finding work that I would be happy to do locally. He was most concerned for the children too, for Jamie entering into what seemed like turbulent teens, and for John-John, so shy and withdrawn, and, of course, Mallika, who might never know a father's love. At the end of our discussions, we felt closer to each other than ever before and very much loved by the other, knowing that we shared each other's most intimate thoughts and feelings.

The inadvertent disclosure of Kumar's letter from Papua New Guinea had started us on this course of open dialogue, without any secrets between us. And now that what we feared was becoming a reality, that openness became the chief ally in our dark tunnel. The children too had become part of all our openness and sharing to the extent that they could assimilate. Slowly, almost miraculously, many friends too became part of our circle, sharing our agony, and sharing their faith with us. The true significance of all this was yet to emerge.

It seemed that each day Kumar wus getting stronger. One day, Dr Benjamin Pulimood, the former Director of Christian Medical College and Hospital, came to visit us bringing with him his own brand of warmth and concern. Dr Pulimood was Kumar's professor of Medicine and an old family friend. He jokingly told us of a patient of his who went into hepatic coma twenty-five times and of another to whom it happened only once. "We will never know the answers to so many mysteries," he said. "That is part of faith. That we accept without understanding, that we trust in a heavenly Father who sometimes cannot explain, for we would certainly not understand it if He did." It was faith in a heavenly Father which kept us going through all the rough days.

One special blessing we had at this time was a young boy called Suresh. Suresh was the son of a gardener in Karigiri. He was bright and articulate. Kumar had looked after Suresh's studies for a few years now and he had become a part of our family. Now, at this time of need, Suresh truly became another son to us. He was always beside Kumar, easing his pain by telling him jokes and stories. He was a big brother for Jamie and John, comforting them, helping them look on the positive side of life, and was a tower of strength for me, running errands, and always there beside me for every emergency .

On Christmas morning, we all went to our church, St John's in Vellore. Kumar looked so lovely in his white silk kurta and dhothi and was in excellent spirits. Deep in my heart there lurked a fear. Would this be our last Christmas together? Could this nightmare happen again? Sensing my fears, Kumar held my hand throughout the service. When the time came to walk up to the altar to receive the consecrated bread and wine, Kumar asked the boys if they would join us for a blessing. It is the custom in our church only for the adults to do so, and I wondered if the children would feel embarrassed coming up with us. Jamie and John-John sensed the urgency and a deep need within Kumar for all of us to be together on this special day and readily agreed. "Please God, heal Kumar, and bring new life to him," we prayed.

10. The Second Coma

D r George Kurian reassured us that all Kumar's biochemical tests after he came out of the coma were quite good. There was little chance of an imminent re-occurrence and it seemed that life could return to almost normal. It was the end of the year, we had missed being with my parents for Christmas and so we went to Madras for a reunion with my family.

As both Kumar's parents were dead, my family had become so dear to him, and he had built good loving relationships with my aunts, uncles and cousins. They too cherished him in a special way. This annual family party was something we all looked forward to, and though very tired, Kumar was the life of the party. I was very surprised when, the next day, he plunged into deep depression. We decided to return to Karigiri to be closer to his doctors and to celebrate the New Year. Kumar was so restless. A bad spell of coughing and bouts of severe nausea kept him awake all night. I cradled him in my arms and watched over him, praying for just a few hours of sleep for him. I had a feeling that all was not well with him and decided to take him into hospital in the morning just to check him out. By the time we got there, Kumar was in coma again.

It was exactly two months since the first coma. Coma! An ugly word, that evoked deep fear in all of us. It really means a state of unconsciousness, but to us, it was more than just this. It meant seeing the man we loved lying there so deathly pale, speechless, inert, unable to respond to our voices, to our love and to our touch. Just a few days ago, we were contemplating Kumar returning to work, now we were suddenly plunged into a state of limbo again. Life, it seemed, could be so deceiving and cruel.

It was the end of the year 1996, and all our friends were away. Outside the ICU, I sat alone and numb. I never expected this to happen again so soon. I felt completely isolated.

"Help me Lord," I prayed. "Don't abandon him, don't desert me, help me deal with the guilt that I should have looked after him better. Forgive me for all the times I've been impatient with him. I honestly thought he was getting better."

My faith told me that God was there, but only this time, there were no miraculous assurances, no warmth, just the feeling of being forsaken.

Sometime ago, I had copied out a sentence from Elisabeth Elliot's *A Path Through Suffering* which touched my heart. Now, it surfaced to my mind to give me strength.

"Teach me to treat all that comes to me with peace of soul and with the firm conviction that Your Will governs all. In unforeseen events let me not forget that even this is sent by You."

How do I attain this peace of soul, Lord? At a time like this when everything is collapsing around me, where do I find peace of soul and heart?

The boys were devastated. Jamie put aside his fear and revulsion for hospitals and stayed with me outside the ICU. He had always seen me strong and calm. Now, it distressed him so much to see me weeping and frightened. He put his arms around me and held me tight, as we counted the hours. Watching over Kumar with hope, waiting, praying that he would wake up again.

This time the waking up was even more traumatic. As soon as Kumar was conscious and could look around, he knew what had happened. An agonized scream came from him as he tried to pull out the tubes from his throat and nose in frustration and anger. He had been in a coma for two days, had lost a lot of weight and was extremely weak. The grey and white stubble on his face and the pale yellow colour of his jaundiced eyes gave him a ghostly look. His feet were tied by restrainers and he kicked at them furiously. The transfusion needles pinned to his arm also caused him a great deal of pain. He cried bitterly and reproached me angrily for keeping him in this undignified state. The post-coma trauma of pain, restlessness and relentless nausea was beginning to set in.

"Why? Why? Why?" he cried desperately, again and again in a voice hoarse with pain. I had no answers for his questions. After two days of battling with my own uncertainties, my fears and guilt that I had allowed this to happen to him again, I had no strength to even face him. We just clung to each other and wept. There was a crushing need within both of us for an explanation as to why this had happened again so soon, when all seemed to be going well. I felt like a person betrayed. All my prayers, all my hopes, seemed to crumble. I felt drained and empty inside me.

Seeing my shock and despair, Jamie took over from me this time. He dried his father's tears, and stroked his back, whispering loving words of encouragement all the time. "We're together again, Appa, that's all that matters. This time, we will all take care of you really well so that this won't happen again."

"Just look at me, son, how awful I look."

"You look lovely to me, Appa. I'm so happy to see you. I love you Appa, I just want you to get well and come home again. Does your arm hurt, Appa? Shall I kiss it better for you?"

Kumar nodded his head.

With tears in his eyes, Jamie gently kissed the place around which the needles went in. This was a childhood ritual that Kumar had used on Jamie when he was small and was in pain. Now here he was, using the same 'kiss it better' ritual on his father with great effect.

"Is that better, Appa? Come on now give me a little smile?" Kumar gave a small smile for his son.

Slowly, Jamie fed his father some of the tasteless porridge he was allowed, chatting to him all the while about the antics of his baby sister, and later stroked his arms and his stomach until he fell asleep.

Every time Kumar woke up, Jamie was beside him, loving him, talking to him, whispering words of hope and life. I sat beside Kumar, holding his swollen hand in mine, trying to find words that would ring true. The hardest thing to do right then was to find hope, and yet, hope was all we had to cling to.

Once again, Kumar was back in the medical ward. We were familiar to the nurses and they took extra special care of both of us. The recovery took a little longer this time, for Kumar was weaker than before. I stood outside, silent in sad reflection. It was evening time. The sun was setting and there seemed to be shadows everywhere. Shadows that followed me, shadows that blended into the darkness that was descending from the sky, enveloping me. To get away from this terrible gloom, I went inside and what I saw broke my heart. Jamie was in bed with Kumar, one arm around his head, the other had been stroking his forehead. John-John too was curled up beside him, he had been stroking Kumar's stomach. All three of them were asleep. Kumar's forehead was smooth again after hours of being furrowed in pain. It was such a touching tableau of love.

"Doesn't this get to you Lord?" I asked, "How can you see this and not feel all our pain? How can you see this and not be touched by it? How can you keep healing away from us? I commit my precious darling to you, thank you for his life and all that has been between us. Take care of him, Lord, as he journeys towards you. Hold his hands in yours and give him his faith back. Wrap him up in your presence. Heal him, Please."

I knew Kumar had begun the long journey towards the Valley of the Shadow of Death. Somewhere deep in my soul I knew that God had left me with no other source to depend on this time so that I would learn to depend only on Him. I knew without a doubt that He was preparing me for all that lay ahead, and that frightened me. I thought of the children's sadness and despair, of how unreal our lives were at this moment.

The doctors were now seriously thinking of a liver transplant as the only hope left for Kumar. We were both shattered.

It was the last day of the year 1996. As the hands of the clock sped towards midnight, Kumar and I were wide awake. For a few hours, there had been relief from pain and it was a blessed time. We spoke about all that had happened to us and were deeply thankful that we were still together. I curled up against him in the hospital bed and put my head against his chest. The beat of his heart was rhythmic, familiar and comforting. I couldn't help wondering if we would have another New Year's Eve again. It was, however, not a time for sadness but for giving thanks, for we had truly been blessed in so many ways—with doctors and nurses who took care of Kumar so well, children who were a source of comfort and strength, and friends and family who were caring, loving and supportive.

The children arrived in the morning and decorated the room with colourful balloons and flowers, silent tears flowing down their cheeks. "Happy New Year, Appa," they said and kissed him. We knew the year ahead would bring fears and anxieties that would pierce our hearts, but for now we believed in a 'Happy New Year' for us all. Mallika sitting on Kumar's lap covered his face with kisses. John-John sat curled up beside him, his arms around his father. Jamie sat on the other side holding his hands. Kumar looked happy and relaxed, smothered in the children's love. To celebrate, we had double chocolate ice creams for everyone.

We spoke to Jamie and John-John about the possibility of the transplant and answered all their questions. Initially, they too were distressed as they realized that there was no hope of Kumar getting well on his own. They were both keen that we try every measure possible to save Kumar's life.

Our first visitor in the New Year was a friend of Kumar's who had taken her husband to America for extensive surgery a few years earlier, and whose husband, sadly, died later. She shared with us the agony, the difficulties and expense of such a venture and also the hope and new life that the transplant, if successful, would bring to us. As she was leaving she gave us a folded slip of paper saying, "I hope God will bless this and multiply it for you." It was a cheque for ten thousand rupees.

The hospital expenses and medicines had eaten up most of our savings and even before we could think of the finances needed for such a venture, God was assuring us that He would provide for all our basic needs. Kumar's classmates who were in America had got in touch with one another to look for possible centres where the transplant could be done. It was all rather overwhelming.

New life for Kumar—it should have brought me hope, but it didn't. Deep within me I had this strange feeling that it was not for us. Kumar too felt the same way and, as usual, was the first to voice it to me.

"Is it the huge sums of money involved that's frightening us? Does it mean that we don't trust God enough?" he said.

Our friend's gift was so touching. I opened my Bible to put it away carefully and was amazed when I opened it at the passage of the miracle of the five loaves and two fish. This was the miracle when Jesus blessed a little boy's offering of two fish and five loaves and fed a hungry crowd of five thousand with them. What was God telling us? That He would provide for all our needs? That He would give us a miracle? I had no doubt at all that He would provide for all of our needs and that He would give us a miracle too. But this odd negative feeling inside me still persisted and bothered me.

A new alternative was offered to us—that of having the transplant done here in Vellore itself. No liver transplants had been done here so far, and the infrastructure was not quite ready. But the surgeons, trained abroad, were ready and willing to start. All the medical personnel concerned were confident of success. They just needed a patient who was willing to undergo surgery and a donor. The advantage was that it would be free of cost, all the family could be together and Kumar would get the best of care in every possible way. Kumar was quite certain that he did not want to go abroad leaving the children behind.

"No matter what happens, I want us to stay together. I don't want to die in a strange place, all alone. I don't want the children to face something like this on their own either."

Kumar's moods went up and down, understandably, not just with all these new developments but also with the recurrence of pain. We put forward the idea of having the transplant done in Vellore to Jamie and John-John and they were horrified.

"How could you even think of it, Amma?" said Jamie.

"How could you see Appa as an experiment? If something happened to Appa, people will say you killed him and you won't be able to bear that."

Jamie, as always, was wise and knowing of the world and its ways more than we were, so the question of the transplant being done in Vellore was ruled out. Our families too were totally against the idea and were angry with me for even thinking of it.

We spent a lot of time talking to each other about how much we loved each other and how that love had made each of us independent and strong for the other. Almost two decades of loving, nurturing, cherishing and being there for each other, had made us take it all for granted. Now faced suddenly with the threat of losing it all, what we felt was deep sadness, but not regret. We just held each other close while the tears flowed silently. The tears were often healing too, for we would then remember better times and times of blessing and great joy and end up laughing.

From somewhere in my memory came the phrase "the wound of love." Practice the wound of love. Real love, it is said, hurts. We both knew by now that love had made us open and vulnerable to each other. Love, as we had learnt, had the power to shatter and devastate us. It also had the power to help us heal each other, to be strong for the other despite how weak we felt, and to care for each other no matter what happened.

There were so many prayers for healing. We knew that God could heal Kumar if that was His Will, but we both had the feeling that God wanted to give us something more than just a cure. We spent one sleepless night discussing what it was that God wanted from us.

"Gratitude, trust for whatever happens, an opening of our hearts to His Will, love," said Kumar.

"Funny how love is at the bottom of the list, considering it is the most important commandment," I said, almost in jest and then stopped short, as only that morning I had read a poem that made sense to me now. I fished it out and read it aloud to Kumar.

"I wait for you my child,
I desire your love
More than anything else you can give me.
Not your service,
Not your struggling and trying to please me
Or to please others.
I want you to love me;
To love me with all your heart,
mind, soul and strength.
This is the first commandment
And matters more than all else besides.
I need your love, fellowship and workship,
I want you to be single-minded in this one thing.
My spirit is with you
to empower you,
To fill your heart with love.
I desire this not sometimes,
But always."

There was something He wanted from us. Total love, total commitment. From me, He wanted the complete acceptance that Kumar's life was in His hands. "Thy will be done." It was one thing to say it intellectually, but another to actually accept it and live as though we meant it.

Kumar spoke again of dying in peace, whenever that may be. "When I get to the stage where nothing more can be done for me, please don't let them put me on a ventilator, no drips just to keep me alive in the ICU. I want you to let me go in peace."

I wasn't ready to talk this over, but it was so important to him. To refuse would have been selfish. I had to shelve my own fears and heartbreak and face whatever he wanted to share, with the same dignity and courage that he had.

"I mean it, Ushamma. There will come a time when there will be nothing that anyone can do for me. I want you to promise me that you will allow me to go in peace and that you will be by my side till the end."

Tearfully, I nodded in agreement, although, at that stage, I did not really understand what might be in store for me. Then his mood changed. He hugged me and lifted his eyes above, "Thank you, Lord, for now, for another day just to be together, to share jokes, to laugh, to be able to touch and caress and kiss each other like this."

Soon we were back home in Karigiri again. Many friends came to see us. Although Kumar was in great pain, he put up a brave front and joked with everyone. He looked weak, but he certainly didn't give the impression of a dying man.

The nights continued to be traumatic. As it started getting dark, Kumar began to panic, fearful of going to sleep in case he slipped into another coma. The nausea intensified, the pain was relentless. When we were alone, he pleaded with me for a pain reliever. All pain relievers contained chemicals which would filter through the liver and damage it further. So pain-killers were taboo. I felt so cruel refusing him and he was furious with me. It was as though God was driving sharp nails into my heart the whole time, a little deeper each day.

To make the nights something to look forward to, on sleepless nights, I would light about a dozen scented candles, play some of our favourite music and make us a cup of coffee. Sitting back against our large, fluffy pillows, we would talk about the old days when we were young and when the children were little. It was amazing how the memories which were long forgotten came back to our minds. The memories of sad times, bad times too, helped us realize that God had been faithful and kind to us all through our years together. Often, laughing at something, Kumar would fall asleep peacefully in my arms.

For Kumar, the pain was in his stomach, in his hands and in his feet. For the children and me, the pain was in our hearts. For all our pain, there was no cure, no magic remedy. There is nothing romantic or sweet about pain. To suffer intensely is to see it for what it really is... a dominating, fearful thing. Something that takes over one's entire life, so that you think it, feel it, breathe it and nothing else really matters. One of the blessings for a person in pain is relief from pain, whether for just a few hours or a longer period. Sometimes, it seemed as if all our pain would go on for ever and ever, and then there were times of sudden relief. Those were times of blessedness, of joy, of true thankfulness. We learned to appreciate small things. Just a few hours sleep was something to be thankful for. An hour without pain for Kumar, was something to tell everyone about; a whole morning without pain had me sharing the news with my Mum and Dad in Madras.

So many people came to pray for us. "You must have faith," they said, "Your faith alone can heal him, Usha, you must pray harder." I assured them that I did pray all the time and they looked sceptical. They left me with the terrible feeling that my lack of faith, commitment or prayer or worse, any unconfessed sins, were preventing Kumar's healing.

I knew that God had the power to remove all the pain and heal Kumar completely. I knew of so many to whom this had happened. Yet for some reason, He chose not to heal Kumar. Should we batter heaven's door with loud persistent prayers? Didn't God know the deepest desires of our hearts? Did He want us to crumble and break in despair before He would eventually hear us? Somehow, I didn't think so, yet so often I read the Gospel story of the parable of the woman who pestered the judge and got what she wanted by sheer persistence.

It was confusing. Sometimes, I felt it was easier for some of our visitors to pray for an end to the pain, and give thanks for a miracle than to truly share in our suffering, for that called for time, more openness and more giving of one's self. It was hard for many of our visitors to face the reality of pain and suffering.

"You look great," they would say when Kumar was screwed up in pain. "You'll be back at work in no time at all," when it was so obvious that this would not happen.

One morning, I left Kumar alone for a few minutes and when I returned there were three priests sitting with him praying, "Confess your sins, brother, and the Lord will heal you."

I was so upset. "Please leave him" I pleaded, "he's very tired and ill, he can't take any more of all this."

"Sister, we love him, we want Jesus to heal him. Don't you want him to be healed?" they asked me accusingly.

"Yes, I do, if that is His Will for Kumar."

They left in silence with cold faces and I was left with the guilt of something terrible. Some of these prayers were so loud and long and fervent. Each of these sessions left him weak and angry with God.

"If He won't hear my prayers, won't He atleast hear the prayers of others for me? If He is an all loving God, why doesn't He heal me? How much more does He want from me?" Despair and confusion wrung such heart-rending questions from deep within him.

Faith is certainly needed for healing. So too, I think, is love. Love in the voice of the one who prays, love in the eyes, love in the touch, love in the words spoken. We both knew that not everyone is healed. The Bible clearly says, "Though well attested by faith some did not receive what was promised, since God had foreseen something better for them." (Hebrews 11:39)

What could be better than healing, a return to a wholesome way of life? Those close to us, who prayed in love, prayed, "May Your Will be done in Kumar's life." At times when we experienced this kind of prayer, there was healing of some kind within Kumar, not necessarily relief from pain, but a closeness to God.

11. The Valley Of The Shadow Of Death

It was early January. Winter in Karigiri can be quite chilly. The early morning mist which was thick and grey melted only around ten in the morning. We would sit in the warm sunlight in our garden, play with Mallika and just bask in each other's company. Kumar's brother, Sunder, who had come to visit on hearing that Kumar was ill, stayed on, and often the two brothers reminisced together about their boyhood days.

Two nights after returning home from hospital, the nausea intensified and early in the morning Kumar vomited blood. I was shocked. Within minutes he had a second bleed. He's dying, I thought. The sign of the last stage of liver disease was vomiting blood. I grabbed some clothes and called for the car. My mind flashed back to the letter Kumar had written to me seven years ago. "The end when it comes will be horrible. I will vomit blood and go into a final coma and die."

"Please Lord, let it not end this way, this is his worst nightmare. Let it not come true," I pleaded.

Kumar's voice was calm and strong. "Jamie son, I may not come back again. Take care of Amma for me. Take care of yourself too. Thank you for being such a wonderful son and for all that you have done for me. I love you. Goodbye, son." He gave Jamie a long hug.

Then he pulled John-John towards him. John-John was very special to him in that he was still his baby, and to John he could not speak. He held the weeping little boy against him and kissed him and rocked him in his arms.

Afraid of the time we were wasting, I pulled him away. "Please get in the car, it's getting late." I panicked at all this delay.

Kumar was still so calm, "Give me Mallika, let me kiss her goodbye too." Mallika was asleep in her cradle. I picked her up and gave her to him.

"Bye little darling. God bless you." He put the sign of the cross on her forehead and held her little cheek against his for a few moments. Then he looked around the room, taking it all in as if for the last time. His eyes lingered on the family photographs on the window sill and on the many awards he had received for much of his outstanding work in leprosy.

For the first time, I was weeping. The day was just beginning for everyone else, but for me, life, as I knew it, was ending, for Kumar was dying.

He held me close to him, "It's okay, darling. I'll see you again one day. Be brave."

All the way to the hospital he kept saying, "What a lovely day." And indeed it was. It was seventeen kilometres to the hospital and I was terrified that he would bleed to death before we got there. I asked the driver to drive as fast as he could, but Kumar restrained him, "No, no, this speed is alright. I want to be able to see everything."

It was Pongal, the Tamil season of harvest. The workers were already in the fields, which were like green velvet carpets. The sky too was an extraordinary blue and the air was fresh with the sweetness of the fragrance of the sugarcane harvest. Kumar's eyes drank in the beauty of the morning and this seemed to give him some strength.

We were back in the ICU. The staff were all visibly upset to see us. The nurses came and gave me a hug, "Keep praying," they said.

Kumar had a third bleed. He held my hand and gave a weak sweet smile. "Goodbye, darling. Take care of yourself and the children for me. At all costs, I want you to be happy and to make sure the children stay happy too. Thank you for all that you've done for me. I love you always, in this world and the next."

The nurse tugged at his wedding ring and gave it to me. That seemed to signify the end. Around us there was so much noise. Another patient had been brought into the ICU and the nurses were busy running around trying to organize things for him. I couldn't let Kumar's end be so chaotic and undignified, with so much noise and confusion around us. "At whatever the cost to me, I will grant him the peace and dignity he so wanted," I said to myself, and held his hands.

The nurse drew the curtains around us giving us some privacy. The drips fixed to his arms were causing so much pain, so I borrowed some extra pillows to place under his arm and made him comfortable. I wrapped my soft brown shawl around him to keep him warm, the lingering perfume from it soothed him. Stroking his forehead I sang the twenty-third psalm for him. He closed his eyes and slept for a while, his breathing rhythmic and easy.

The doctors wanted an endoscopy done immediately to check out the bleeding. We had been through this procedure so many times before and it should have only taken a few minutes, but this time it took an hour. An hour in which all I heard was Kumar's strangled screams. The nurses rushed in and out of the endoscopy room, their faces set grimly, not saying a word, not even looking at me.

I felt so alone, helpless and abandoned. No amount of prayer had helped. Heaven was silent again. If there was a heaven. I laid my head on the empty trolley in front of me, oblivious to everything else, feeling empty, frozen, alone. All around me people were milling about, for this was a busy hospital, but none of it touched me. Somebody tapped on the shoulder and said, "Don't cry, God is great." I looked up and saw a person I had never seen before. This was the worst I had ever felt, unconnected to anything or anyone, completely disillusioned. I had given up all hope of healing, of life even, and I seemed to be falling into a pit which was bottomless. All I could feel was darkness and silence. Where were all the promises of strength and of God's presence during times of peril?

From deep within me, my soul cried out, "My God, My God, why have you forsaken me?"

My mind replied, "Because He wasn't there in the first place." A line from Shakespeare's *King Lear* came to mind.

"As flies to wanton boys are we to the Gods, they kill us for their sport."

Was God playing around with me? Was He just testing my faith? Was He watching over me in spite of what I felt? It mattered not. It was all over anyway.

Kumar's scream's from the endoscopy room had petered out and there was silence, the silence of death, I thought. I steeled myself, expecting to see a body covered with a white sheet, when, quite unexpectedly, the nurses wheeled Kumar out again and into the ward. He was weak and pale, and still alive, but for how much longer? His arm had been cut to put in a drip, he throbbed with pain. The antibiotics had to be injected every four hours. More pain. Insulin had to be pumped into him. More pain. He had to have a bowel wash every five hours. More pain and humiliation.

"Just how much can one human being take?" I cried out to no one in particular. The corner room, in which we were, was newly painted and had a picture on the wall, with a verse from Psalm 34.

"I sought the Lord and He answered me;

He delivered me from all my fears."

Kumar looked at the verse and began to cry, "None of it is true, I've cried to Him and prayed and He has not answered me. How can you mock me like this? Take it away. There is no bloody God."

He was so agitated by this verse on the wall that I tried to remove it, but the picture was too high, so it remained where it was, taunting him, mocking him.

Kumar was not just very ill, he also felt betrayed and hurt that the God whom he had trusted and obeyed all his life, could in the end abandon him like this. So many prayers, so much hope, so much faith. It seemed that it had all gone to waste.

Sitting beside Kumar I felt all used up, like an old towel that had been wrung out again and again. All around me I heard the soft whispers of prayer. I closed my ears to it. No more. There was nothing left inside me anymore. Now it was just Kumar and me. A lifetime serving God, obeying Him, had brought us to this. The boys visited in the evening. They too looked pale and ill, their eyes swollen and red from crying.

Kumar now feared everything. "I'm afraid, I'm afraid," he cried, "of pain, of death, of dying. I'm afraid of living, of going on like this. What will happen to me next? Where is God in all this?"

This was the weakest I too had been, my weeping just hadn't stopped. Until this point, I had been so strong and able to cope. Now, I too was filled with dread and fear, for every day brought fresh terrors, new agonies and uncertainties. Our friend and physician, Dr George Kurian, had been away on holiday and was unaware of Kumar's deterioration. He was due back the next day.

"I'm dreading seeing George," said Kumar. Once more the panic and the pain within him had started. I held Kumar in my arms all through the night. He was warm, worn out, but he was still mine.

"Why is God keeping me alive? Of what use am I like this to Him? Where is He?" These tortured questions were wrenched out of him so many times that night. They were my questions too and for a while I had no answers for him. I sat with my head on his lap, as wretched and tormented as he was.

Then from somewhere deep inside me, I got the strength to reply. I realized that the voice was mine, but not the words. "Look at all the people who care for you, who visit, who pray, you're precious to them, sweetheart, you're precious to me, you are very precious to the boys and Mallika. You're precious to God too. For some reason He wants you alive. You are still His child and He has a plan for you. He loves you through all this. He has always loved you, but for now, for some reason, it involves all this pain and suffering. What all this means I don't know, I only know that we must accept it as from Him and trust that He has a purpose for it."

Our pastor from St. John's Church, Vellore, came to be with us that morning. "Kumar, I am going to anoint you with holy oil" said Reverend Sunderarajan. "We will pray that God will heal you through the oil."

"Do what you like, pastor, God doesn't seem to hear our prayers, so oil me, boil me, do anything you like to me. Just make the pain go away." Kumar lay back wearily on his pillow.

Pastor had brought some oil which had been consecrated at the altar, and massaged the oil on Kumar's head to relieve him of his headache, on his arms where the wound from the drip was, on his forehead which hurt, on his stomach which was bloated, on his legs which were swollen, and prayed for healing. My mind just switched off. I had heard these prayers so often, it no longer meant anything to me.

"Fill their hearts with Your peace," prayed the pastor, "and grant them Your strength."

Almost as an instant answer, a feeling of calmness filled my agitated heart, and I was drawn against my wishes into concentrating on the pastor's prayer. I found myself praying for peace for Kumar too. For strength for both of us and the obedience to accept God's Will for us, whatever that may be.

During the prayer, I noticed that Dr George Kurian had slipped into the room quietly. Pastor asked George to take some oil and anoint Kumar, to be part of the healing process. The quietness, the sacred oil, the prayers, all played their part and the gloom within me began to lift. The empty frozen feeling had melted away and there was a kind of peace in my heart. A thankfulness that we had made it through the night to another day.

Kumar saw George and smiled. All the apprehensions he had about meeting George had diffused too. George's visit was a long one.

"This is the Valley of the Shadow of Death you're going through, my friend," he said sadly.

It was the first time I had heard that expression used in connection to us. I knew it to be true. I could see now why God had isolated me, had removed all my crutches, had broken me until I had none to cling to but Him. The Valley of the Shadow of Death was frightening. I anticipated coldness, darkness, loneliness and unbearable grief at the end of it.

Keeping watch through the night now took on a new meaning. The hours between one and four at night were so frightening, so unbearably lonely and so long. I could see now why Jesus needed special strength during those early hours, for it is then that we are most vulnerable to doubt and despair and fear. Waiting for what was to happen the next day, dreading the pain, wanting the cup to pass away from him. Thus does He also understand our loneliness, our fears, our pain. And yes, He too felt the sting of being abandoned by God, though He was the Son of God. It all took on a new meaning now.

It was unnerving not knowing what tomorrow would bring. How much pain? What would happen to Kumar? what would the doctors decide on tomorrow? Where would we be? We had no control over our lives at all.

This disease had driven us from being "givers" to being "receivers." We were at the end of so much love, hugs, visits, gifts of flowers, fruit and little envelopes of money. At first, it was humiliating to be at the receiving end of so much love and so many gifts, but then it made us feel humble and very, very special. For some reason, love and pain went hand in hand in our lives.

I was aware of the need now to prepare myself and Kumar for the inevitable end. "Dear Lord, with all my heart I commit my darling to you. Don't abandon him, give him back his faith. Grant me the love and patience and tenderness to see him through till the end. Please grant me the strength, remove from me my own fears, be with the children and help them to understand all this too."

Kumar's younger sister, Vasantha, flew down from Thailand to be with him. Kumar wept in her arms. A year ago he had been with Vasantha in London, enjoying her home and the delightful company of his teenage nieces. Here he was now weak and dying. There would be no more joyful reunions with them.

Kumar was due for another endoscopy the next day and the memory of the previous one made him double up in pain and fear. There was no way I could calm or comfort him that night. The only relief came from cursing

God, which worried me, and at crucial times my patience, too seemed to snap, which upset me so much.

Kumar was wheeled down to the endoscopy room the next morning. The medical ward has a quiet garden set in a quadrangle inside the hospital. Pretty shrubs, wild jasmine and srnall clusters of colourful flowers helped soothe my mind as I sat in the pale morning sunlight. It had been a long night and it was going to be an even longer day if Kumar was in pain and could not sleep.

"I honestly can't feel you now, Lord, you seem so far away, almost non-existent. But my faith tells me you are here near me. Help me to float on the faith of others who pray for us, who know we are in Your hands. Especially, carry Kumar in Your arms, remove his fears and his pain. Grant him a measure of Your peace. Grant him healing. In Your name I ask," I prayed.

I read the rest of Psalm 34. It had become my psalm for this time.

"The Lord is close to those whose courage is broken,
And He saves those whose spirit is crushed."

Certainly, I qualified for this psalm, for my courage was broken and my spirit was crushed. The endoscopy was less painful than the previous time and Kumar was anxious to be with his brother and sister.

Vasantha and Sunder spent a lot of time with him that day, cheering him up by reminiscing over their childhood days. I went home in the afternoon. The familiar surroundings, our bed, my dressing table with the bottles of perfume and after shave, all made me feel how unreal our lives were at this moment.

The clothes that Kumar had last worn were still on the bed. As I folded them, the fragrance of his after shave wafted out, and I realized that for so long the only smell I could recognize was that of hospital antiseptic. My heart was breaking, aching. I just sat there weeping at all that had happend to us. Although I was deeply aware of God's presence at so many times during Kumar's illness, I also felt abandoned at times. I was also very afraid. Afraid of all the changes, afraid of all the responsibilities now thrust upon me, afraid of the future. There were lots of questions too. Will I have patience? Will I be able to cope? What effect will all this have on me? I was also very lonely. There was no one to put their arms around me and say, "Don't worry, everything will be okay." Often I felt cold and empty inside me and now especially, I was so desperate for love and warmth and anything that brought promises of life to me.

Mallika, playing outside, peeped through the window, calling, "Amma, Amma, Amma," in her lilting baby voice.

I was surprised as it was the first time she had called me "Amma" and I had been longing to hear those words from her. I went outside to pick her up. She stood in front of me, wide-eyed, a beaming smile on her face, her hands behind her back, and suddenly she thrust a huge yellow flower at me. "Amma," she said again and jumped into my arms. A moment ago, I was crying and thinking how terrible my life was, and now, here I was, laughing with my precious little girl. The pain had given way to such joy and I was so conscious of it.

Mallika's first gift to me came at a time when I so badly needed to know that I was loved and that there would still be love in my life after Kumar was gone. All I could feel was pure joy, coloured yellow from the beautiful flower she gave me, and warmth. A few moments ago, I thought the pain and sadness would never go away, now here I was, bubbling with joy inside me.

It seemed that joy and sadness often come together. It is when we are truly in pain that we know what joy is and true joy often comes in the form of a smile, a hug, or just a baby's first word. The words of my favourite hymn came to mind,

"O joy that seekest me through pain,
I cannot close my heart to Thee,
I trace the rainbow through the rain,
And feel the promise is not vain,
That morn shall tearless be."

There was more excitement over the transplant. Kumar's sister and brother helped to push the idea into some kind of reality. Kumar's classmates in the U.S. were also responding with names of centres where the transplants were being done and of specialist surgeons. They had also set up a fund to collect the huge sums of money that were necessary for the transplant. Kumar was not at all convinced that it was the right thing for him, but it seemed churlish and ungrateful to rebuff everyone's concern and help. We prayed again for guidance. After many days we had a good night's sleep.

Our return home this time was wonderful. Mallika was so excited to see Kumar, she came straight from her potty much to everyone's amusement. Kumar didn't care, he wanted her in his arms anyway.

By now Kumar was so weak and frail. Another bleed could happen anytime without warning. The anger that this was happening to him just kept increasing. All this while he had been fighting, accepting that all this pain, suffering and humiliation was God's final will for him—not being famous, or winning the Nobel prize for achievements in leprosy. There were a lot of restrictions in what he could do now. He needed help getting up and sitting down. Most of the time, he was too weak to even feed himself.

A glance into the mirror brought on a fresh wave of anger and despair. Dressing well, looking good and being well groomed were always an important part of his life. He had a large collection of shirts from all over the world and now he was reduced to wearing just the largest and the most shapeless of them. His appearance too had changed. He looked gaunt and thin. All the muscle from his arms and legs had wasted away. His stomach was round and bloated. His eyes were a pale yellow. He wept at the sight of himself. "Why is God doing this to me? Why is He taking everything that was important to me away from me?"

A large part of the anger too was knowing that he might never get back to work again and that he could not make anymore contributions to the fight against leprosy. All rhe images he had of himself—the self- esteem, the pride in being husband, father, provider, resourceful friend, scientist—had slowly blurred into nothing. All that was left was a blind rage that this could happen to him.

The news of the transplant got more and more hopeful. One evening, the president elect of the American Leprosy Missions, Mr Edgar Stoez, visited us at home. After chatting to Kumar about leprosy for a while, he stunned us with his news. He had a friend who worked in the Pittsburgh Liver Transplant Unit in America and seemed hopeful that he could help get a concession on the finances, find us a place to stay and help put us on a priority list.

Mr Stoez's visit was unnerving in that, once more, everything seemed to be out of our hands. Decisions were being made for us by others. I knew that if this was what God wanted for Kumar, it would all fall into place and it looked as if it was falling into place. Was this to be the miracle that we had all prayed for? The children and the rest of the family were so excited. For the first time, everything seemed so hopeful and positive—the finances, the centre, the place for us to stay, plus a guardian angel in the form of Edgar Stoez who would look after everything for us. A successful transplant could give Kumar a new life span of at least fifteen years. He could get back to work, travel again and life would become the way it used to be before this nightmare started. That night, as usual, we had our family prayers on our bed. The children read a passage from the Bible. Mallika fooled around in Kumar's arms and he taught her to say, "Thank you Jesus. Amen." Then he prayed for guidance. "Lord, we commit all our plans to you. The odds seem against us, but we know that if this transplant is Your Will for me, then we have nothing to fear. I ask You now to show me clearly that this is Your Will. If it is not, please show us that too."

Kumar then put Mallika to sleep in his arms and we chatted about all the new developments.

"Are you still apprehensive, still afraid?" he asked me.

"Yes. For some reason God has withheld healing from you. The eyes of so many people are on us, watching us, seeing how we are coping with all the disappointment. Waiting to see if we will really accept His Will in our lives, or if we will give up at the last moment. I know that this is a great testing time for us, the pain, the uncertainty, and now this offer from Mr Stoez is rather bewildering. I don't know what God wants from us. I only know that He will show us the way."

12. An Act Of Defiance

Two hours after we had prayed for guidance, I was back outside the ICU for the fourth time in two months. Kumar had slipped into a third coma. The night air was cold, the wind cutting into my face as I sat in the familiar place on the floor outside the ICU.

"Lord, I know we asked you for guidance, but I never imagined you would hear our prayers so fast, or answer us in such a dramatic way." I realized then that answered prayers are scary. It was almost as if God was saying, "You asked for it, and I've given it to you. Now that you've got what you wanted, what are you going to do with it?"

I knew that I was losing Kumar and that the end was approaching fast. There was no one with me as I sank to my knees on the cold, stone floor. "Please be with my darling, Lord. Keep him with you." The next few words stuck in my throat. I just could not say what I needed to say. I needed to say "Your Will Lord, not mine, where his life is concerned."

For seven long years, from the time I read the letter he had written in Papua New Guinea, I had prayed for healing for Kumar, and it was with great sadness that l accepted that this was not to be. Now, not only did I have to accept that there would be no miraculous healing for Kumar, but l had to release him and all that l held dear into God's hands and allow Him to do what He thought was best for Kumar. I realized that once I said that prayer, there was no going back.

I sat there for a long while, battling with myself, and finally said, "Your Will, Lord, not mine." There were no more tears, there was no anger, no bitterness. The sweet words of an old hymn surfaced to my mind to strengthen me.

"When Peace like a river attendeth my way,
When sorrows like sweet billows roll,
Whatever my lot, Thou hast taught me to say,
It is well, it is well with my soul."

The peace that had eluded me for so long wrapped itself around me. Warm and comforting. I felt cocooned in a special kind of heat which I called grace and peace. To others, it may have seemed like numbness or shock. But to me the Peace was a gift from God.

Kumar woke up two days later to such pain and fury. "Why did you bring me out of the coma?" he cried pathetically. "How much pain do you want me to go through? You know that there is nothing that can be done for me now. Please, let me go in peace. Take me out of here, I want to go home. I want to die at home."

He was so agitated that they moved him from the ICU into the ward again quickly. He had lost so much weight in these last two days. His arms were swollen from the cuts made to insert the drip. His stomach was bloated, his feet were even more swollen than before. The pain of seeing each other like this was tearing us both apart.

He caressed my face so gently in spite of all his pain, "My poor Ushamma, what a lot I've put you through. How unfair I've been on you. How much I love you. Just promise me one thing now, no more of this. You know I can't take it any more. I want to die at home, in your arms and in dignity. Please do this for me."

I nodded my assent tearfully. Now at peace, he slept for a while as I sat and watched over him.

The enormity of the promise I had just made began to sink into me and I was terrified. The Chief of Medicine, Dr Dilip Mathai, came on his rounds in the evening. Kumar told him that the next time he went into a coma he did not want to be brought to hospital. Neither did he want to be forcibly revived. Dr Mathai, an old friend, held Kumar's thin frail hands in his own strong ones and spoke gently to him. "Kumar, I know the pain is more than you can bear, and perhaps now is not the time to talk about this, but we have to do all that we need to do to keep you alive. We cannot not treat you."

Most doctors know that they cannot afford to have their patients lose hope, even when it is obvious that they are dying. The doctor himself is the source of the patient's hope and therefore his reaction to his patient's request either offered hope or subtly took it away. Dr Mathai was aware of this.

"I know. But this is something which I have thought about for the last two months. I want to be able to decide for myself how to spend the days left to me. Please understand, I am not asking to die. I want to live, and I want to live as best as I can under the circumstances. You and I know that my end is near. I want to go home, I want to spend what little time I have with Usha and the children. I want to make plans, to prepare them for what must be. I think l have that right and the responsibility. Usha has agreed that the next time I go into a coma, I will not be brought to hospital and that she will look after me at home."

Dr Mathai looked at me. I nodded my agreement. He looked shocked. Still holding Kumar's hands he looked straight at him and said "'Okay, Kumar, I respect your wishesl But I need to talk to Usha too."

He led me outside. "This has been a terrible ordeal for you. Does Kumar mean what he says, or is it that the pain is too much right now?"

"Kumar mean what he says, it's something we've discussed for a while and l've promised, to stay beside him and give him all the support he needs."

Thus was the decision made.

Dr Anand Zachariah who had been Kumar's physician for many years, and who had seen us through so many ordeals, also understood and respected Kumar's wishes. "Kumar, I will be there for you to ensure that all goes well," he said. "Even if you don't come into hospital, please remember that l am still here for you, and that l will do all I can to help you through this painful time."

Kumar called for Dr Fritchi and Uncle Zachariah, old and trusted friends, and Dr Job, his grand-uncle, and told them of his decision. All of them looked utterly shocked and pained.

"You know that the end is approaching fast, I want to be at home and enjoy what little time I have. I need you to promise me that you will stay with Usha and see her through this."

Sadly, they all gave their consent, hoping that this was just the confusion caused by the coma.

There was a calm after all the excitement and Kumar slept for a while. Dr George Kurian too had heard of Kumar's decision and came to see him. Kumar was asleep so the two of us sat outside and relived the day's events. George hid his face in his hands and wept, "How am I going to say goodbye to him?" After a while, he dried his eyes, and said, "What can we do to make his last days happy? I know Kumar so badly wanted a few days at the beach with you and the children. Would you like me to take a few days off and come with you?"

I was used to George's kindness and love, but inspite of it, I was moved by his offer.

Kumar woke up and was delighted to see his friend. Gone was the tiredness and the pain. They swapped bawdy jokes and old college stories. Kumar teased the nurse on duty, and me, relentlessly, and was in high spirits. He ordered coffee for everyone late in the night and it was party time in his room. Besides George and me, there was Dr Selvashekar, his young colleague and friend from Karigiri, Dhanajayan, who was a lorry driver and a special friend, and Inba, the lab technician who used to draw blood from him for all his tests. All three had enjoyed a special relationship with Kumar in the past, and had been beside him since he fell ill in October. Now they were like brothers to him, humouring him, sharing his pain, listening to him and just being there for him.

At exactly midnight, Kumar said, "George, I want to go home now. Right now. And no one is going to stop me."

He had had enough of discomfort and pain. Of the indignities caused by bowel washes, needles and drips into his veins, of painful injections, tasteless hospital food, and coarse white sheets. He was angry with God for having betrayed him, for withholding healing from him and for keeping him alive under these terrible circumstances. He was resentful of fate for having dealt him an unfair hand. Thus, choosing the time and manner of his leaving the hospital was a last act of defiance and self-assertion on his part. An angry determination to die as he chose, if he could not live as he wished. In frustration, he pulled out all the needles and drips from his arm, and with great effort, he got out of bed and walked to the wheel chair.

So that's what we did. We got ourselves discharged at midnight much to everyone's dismay.

Kumar could not sleep once we returned home. The boys were concerned over our sudden return and humoured Kumar by watching a couple of movies with him until five in the morning and then, exhausted, they all fell asleep for a while.

13. In Acceptance Lies Peace

The next day was Sunday. I called Dr Fritschi, a previous Director of Karigiri, and an old friend, who was also a priest, to tell him that we were now home. Kumar, dressed in his favourite red shirt, sat outside in the garden. His arm throbbed with pain, his heart was torn between the anger at being reduced to this state of weakness and sickness and the pain of knowing that his end was now imminent. Both these feelings made him withdraw from me while I bathed him and helped him to dress that morning.

My heart was breaking. Because I loved him so much, and could not bear to see him so tormented and destroyed, I had agreed to a course of action over which I knew I would have little control. What I did not expect was his aloofness from me. It terrified me. At that moment, there was no one I could share something so personal with, so I cried while I was having my bath and prayed desperately for strength. I had no idea how I would get through the day.

It was Sunday, a day when Christians usually celebrate the ritual of Holy Communion. In it, we share consecrated bread and wine. These are symbols of the breaking of Christ's body and the shedding of His blood when He was crucified. In the Communion, we not only remind ourselves of the sufferings of Jesus, but also renew our faith. To many, the act of Communion brings healing and hope when they feel broken and lost.

Dr Fritschi and his wife, Aunty Mano, arrived with bread and wine and asked if Kumar would like a service of Communion. Apart from our family, others whom we loved were also unexpectedly there that morning—Uncle and Aunty Zachariah, Vasantha and Sunder, Suresh and a few other friends and helpers. All my yellow flowers were in full bloom, the sky was a bright blue and it seemed that all the birds in Karigiri were singing in our garden that morning. The air was warm and fragrant with the perfume of flowers. There outside, surrounded by so much colour and beauty and love, we had a small service of unction—a service where the sick person is anointed with holy oil.

DrFritschi explained to us that he was going to anoint Kumar with holy oil and pray for "healing or release." He asked us also to participate in this action. Reverently, we dipped our fingers in the oil, and tenderly and gently laid our hands on Kumar. This was not a magical gesture, but an act of consecration, which said,

"Lift up your soul, Kumar, lift it up to the Lord. Stop struggling, feel His warmth and peace. Let it flow into you. We love you. Feel our love as we lay our hands on you and be healed of all that is tearing you apart. Allow the love and peace of God to flow into you and be healed."

Each of us in our hearts lovingly committed Kumar to God, and asked for healing for him or release from all his pain and suffering. Perhaps the sensation of tender touch and the recognition of loving hearts united in one prayer communicated more effectively than words to him. For in that symbolic act, all of us there, even those who did not share our faith, became physical channels of a spiritual experience for Kumar, a moment of experiencing 'God's presence with the skin on.' When every hand laid lovingly on him truly became the hand of God.

The small group of people gathered together in our garden that morning included those who truly believed in the Christian faith, those of other faiths, and some who had no religious faith at all. Yet everyone wanted to be beside Kumar to share in his suffering, to pray for healing or release from all his pain. Thus, in doing so, gathering together with one aim, and in great love, we were also able to draw closer to one another, irrespective of the differences in our faith, our status and the other usual barriers which separate people.

It was love that helped us to unite our deepest selves in this way. Through this love and unity that we experienced, we became aware of the hidden presence of God in each of us. The presence of God was not just in our hearts, but also in our hands when we reached and touched Kumar. It surrounded us, upholding Kumar in his brokenness and all of us in our despair.

After the anointing, the simple yet familiar words of the Communion service reached out to Kumar even more. After the service his face was radiant. Gone was the tension, the pain, the fear and the terrible anger that had been part of his life for so long. In his heart he had finally accepted that this was God's Will for him. He was able to pray and commit his tormented spirit and his worn out body to God—"Your Will Lord, not mine, and if that means you withhold healing from me and take me away from my family and all that I hold dear, then so be it." As he voiced this prayer in his heart, peace settled on him so beautifully.

Later that evening, Kumar said to me, "As I sat in the garden drenched with so much beauty and love, I felt God's hand on me. I felt Him cradling me, calling me, reassuring me of His presence and His love, and it was impossible not to respond to that love. This was the God who has been with me all through my life. I knew that I could trust Him to lead me to my end."

The service in the garden was a turning point for both of us and the children. Just as Kumar felt the hand of God on him, and was filled with peace, I too felt the reassuring presence of God. An hour earlier, the sadness, the fear, and the loneliness of being in this situation was tearing me apart. Now, a feeling of calmness and strength descended on me. I knew that I would be able to cope with the uncertainties and pain of the days ahead.

Kumar looked so beautiful, full of smiles and filled with love, and this love made him glow. The boys were too young to understand the significance of this service, but they knew that their father had finally made his peace with God. They could see for themselves how his face shone with happiness and love. How he held on to me and caressed my fingers and my face. The thought of losing Kumar terrified them. Death, loss and grief were strangers to us till now. But for the moment, their fears were bound up, as they too were filled with peace, strength and love. Kumar's joy was reflected in their faces and in their eagerness to please him and make him happy.

Both of us were filled with a sense of urgency from then on, there was not a moment to lose or waste. Every hour counted. Each hour was to be a celebration of life and something special. Kumar had always wanted to see Mallika with earrings and I had evaded the issue as I felt that she was too young for them. Now, it was important to me that he had the simple pleasure of seeing his daughter with earrings on. So I called up someone who was willing to pierce her ears at home and we had it done within the hour. He was delighted to see her looking so cute and feminine.

There was no more pain to endure because whenever the pain started I could now give him a pain killer to relieve it. Kumar's decision not to go back to hospital for active treatment, and his resolve to face his end on his terms, meant that many of the earlier restrictions like being on a special low protein diet, and avoiding pain-killers which would have further damaged his liver, were now lifted. The boys stayed back from school and spent all their time at his side. In some ways, it was the happiest time of our lives, and in some ways, also the saddest.

Many people wanted to know why God had sent this disease on Kumar, who had always done good and helped so many people, who had so much to give to the leprosy world, and who had a full life ahead of him. Through his acceptance of his disease, Kumar had come to realize that this period of sickness was a test, not so much of what happened to him, but how he dealt with it.

"It was not my business to ask why or even expect an answer. I was to accept it all in faith that this was part of God's plan for me. For me, as a Christian, this was most important," he said to those who could not understand why this had happened to him. "For some reason God has brought me to this point. All my research contributions, all the travel, the fame and honours bestowed on me, were His gifts to me. So too was this suffering, and really it was this gift of suffering that brought me back to Him."

One evening after a long period of reflection he said, "I realize I have been through a period of pruning when God has stripped me of everything I once held important. My job, my status, my looks, everything is being taken away slowly. Yet, even as I lose it all, and as I mourn for it, there is now also a richness and beauty in my life, and a love that I would never have known otherwise."

Our mornings were spent in the garden which we both loved and had once tended with such care. Sitting in the warm sunshine, holding his hands, caressing his face, became for me the happiest moments of the day. Often, he would share with me something which he had meditated on during his prayer time.

"Jesus died of something He didn't deserve," he said to me one morning as we sat out in the sun. "Jesus who always did good suffered terribly too, without pain-killers, and was lonely and afraid at the end, just like me, so He really understands what I've been through and what I am about to go through too." Such reflections helped me too. We leaned on each other, offering strength to each other for the difficult days ahead.

As a family we began to see the many facets of healing—the miracle that we had all prayed for. But people's minds were usually fixed only on physical healing.

"What does healing really imply?" Kumar asked a colleague who was crying for him. "Freedom from pain? A reversal or halt of the disease? A return to the kind of life I lived before? All that is healing of a kind, yes. Yet there is a healing that is much more miraculous and necessary for life—a healing of our whole being. A healing of our twisted emotions, bitter feelings, and unresolved anger. That is the healing that I am experiencing now, the acceptance and the release of all that has been suppressed and hidden inside me for so many years."

"How do you know this for sure?" asked the same colleague.

"Because there is absolute peace in my heart, in spite of all the sadness and pain. This continuous peace and joy in my heart is the sign that I have truly been healed."

Much healing also came from the caring hands and presence of both our doctors, George Kurian and Anand Zachariah. Building on the rapport and trust which had taken years to establish, they now took on the burden of weeping with those who wept and waiting with those who waited.

Many doctors avoid getting involved with their patients. For, what kind of a message does it convey when a doctor breaks down in sadness and helpless in front of his patient? George and Anand, by choosing to share in our suffering, by spending time with us and talking to us, became channels of healing. By taking on so much of our pain, they helped to untangle many of Kumar's confused thoughts and fears. When their medical expertise had been depleted, they stayed on beside us to ease the loneliness of sleepless nights. They listened, they held his hands, and finally they gave him strength to negotiate life on his own terms.

Dying with dignity became Kumar's chief concern. As a scientist, he had been the kind of person who was meticulous about procedure, about adequate preparation and the end results. He applied the same attitude now towards dying.

First, there were basic needs that had to be met, like keeping him clean and warm, seeing that he still looked and smelled good, helping him with the elimination of bodily wastes, keeping him free from pain and the restlessness which bothered him so much. He knew that these simple needs would be well taken care of by me. Both his doctors promised him that they would see to it that he would not scream or groan in pain, by prescribing mild sedatives to keep him calm. Kumar was happy with the drugs they prescribed, and was reassured by their promises. Knowing that there would be no painful struggles and knowing that he would be kept comfortable meant so much to him.

Now that some aspects of the outward dignity that was so important to him while dying was assured, he felt relieved and could now concentrate on things that really mattered to him.

We knew that Kumar could slip into a final coma at any time without warning, so we learned to live one day at a time. Kumar was insistent on speaking of the future without him. Both Jamie and John-John had stayed back from school to be with him during these last days, so Kumar wanted them both to repeat the year at school.

It was a time of intense sharing, and last minute advice. "It will be a year of such changes for you all, and the last thing you should do is nag the children about their studies. You should build your relationship with them, spend time with them, grieve with them, take them out, do special things with them. They have one else but you from now on," he said to me.

"You must keep yourself busy and do things which will bring you a measure of happiness too. I know you will miss me, but there will come a time when your life will move on and I will become just a memory."

Not knowing if Kumar would have another day made each day so special for us. Nothing was put off until tomorrow. We looked through all our old photograph albums with the children and laughed at all the memories of the times when they were small. We had a last game of scrabble, we listened to our favourite songs, I cleared out my wardrobe and spread out all the saris he had bought me over the years for him to see again.

One night, I opened a bottle of wine that I had saved for a special occasion. The boys laid the table outside on the verandah, lit tall, fragrant candles, and put out our best china. I wore Kumar's favourite sari, a green and gold one that he had given me at the time of our engagement. He was so surprised and thrilled by this gesture. It was to be a romantic meal for just the two of us, but the children couldn't bear to be left out, so they joined us too. So did my mother and Kumar's brother. I wanted some privacy, a little time for one last romantic memory. It seemed that everyone wanted a memory of Kumar enjoying the wine, sitting under the stars, looking so peaceful and beautiful.

Much later that night we had our time together. "Poor Ushamma, you've been dealt such an unfair deal in life. I can never forget how you've been so wonderful, so beautiful, caring and supportive of me all this while. Never leaving my side, understanding me, loving me through everything. It is by the grace of God that I have been given you. Whenever I have wondered why, why me, I have also seen the blessings and the gift of you for me, and the wonder of our marriage, especially now. It could not have been otherwise, and I am so thankful for everything." This too was part of the healing.

The days that followed were happy and full of love. As we sat out in the sun every morning, enjoying the birds and the flowers, I thought of all the pain we had been through to come to this point. Often, we did not say anything to each other. Words were no longer necessary. Just the look in our eyes said it all. God in His mercy often,

"lent us an hour for peace and for forgetting, and set in pain the jewel of His joy."

Kumar's aunts, who were all in their eighties, travelled a long way to visit him. It was a happy reunion, when they affectionately brought out precious memories of a fond nephew.

Friends came from all over the country to sit beside him for just a while, and to say farewell. It was a time of rejoicing. It was also a time when we felt the kindness and the support of a loving Christian community around us. In the face of human tragedy, people are somehow galvanized to rally around. So many friends and members of our Church in Vellore sent boxes of tasty food for the family, and special treats for Kumar and the children, knowing that it was a difficult time for the boys. Every Sunday, the beautiful flowers from the altar at our church were sent to us with a message from whoever arranged them. "Our thoughts are with you. We love you."

Calls and letters full of love started to arrive from all over the world. "Miracles are in His hands, but brotherhood He has given us as a right," wrote Gunnar from Norway, reassuring us that Kumar was indeed a beloved brother to him. Louisa, from Fiji, sent a large heart-shaped love cake so that Kumar could eat it and enjoy the memories of his time with them in Fiji. From Singapore, friends called everyday. Kumar's classmates from other countries called often, offering words of comfort and hope. His friends from Vellore visited often, bringing their lunch with them, so that they could spend a little extra time with him.

Kumar was his usual jovial self, chatting to his visitors about the everyday concerns of life, and also about his faith, his needs and his end. By being open with each other and the children, sharing our feelings, our fears and our concerns, we had drawn closer to each other during this period. Now, we were just as transparent with our friends, and many were drawn to us by this openness and the intimacy it offered. Often in the evenings, they brought a special dish and stayed to eat with us. Nobody felt that they were intruding or that they were loading me with extra work. We discovered that a meal together, under these circumstances, was both sacred and intimate. Around the table, we became a family, a small community, one body, held together by immense suffering, sadness and love.

By confronting death within himself and by talking about it to me and the children, Kumar had come face to face with the ultimate enemy of life. Once he had done this, all barriers were broken down. He knew what he wanted, and how he wanted to live the days granted to him.

Some well-wishers who came to share in our sadness, also became drawn into this atmosphere of openness and closeness, and, in the process, became very dear to us at this time. This was particularly enriching for Kumar, as he felt that even in his dying, he was able to reach out to people, and still have a meaningful relationship, without all the preliminaries of getting to know a person.

Death is a taboo topic in our society, possibly abetted by the superstitious belief that to talk about something bad is to encourage it to happen. So by talking about it openly and honestly, Kumar broke the ultimate of barriers. As friends became involved with our struggle, they too somehow felt enriched by Kumar's openness in talking about death, and in his facing it positively, almost joyously. For we realized that in looking at death squarely, and right in the eye, we are better able to face life positively, to draw closer to one another, to look inside ourselves, rearrange our priorities and be happy and thankful for every day and the many blessings it brings. Kumar's dying and his positive attitude towards it, helped us all to be more 'alive' in many ways. Alive in the sense that to some, it was the deepening of their faith, for others it was the exposure to the ultimate issues of existence—What is the meaning of life? Who am I really? Why is this happening to me? Where is God in all this? This unusual exposure at this time and in this setting, in an ambience of faith, hope and love, heightened a sensitivity which allowed them to explore and find the core of their own spirituality. That core or depth in one's own being where one meets the image of God.

For many of Kumar's medical friends caught up in a culture where life is reduced to a heartbeat and a brainwave, this almost joyful acceptance of death brought frustration and helpless at first. Then came a period of intense reflection as they grappled with their own attitudes to life and faith.

Mary Ganguly, Kumar's classmate wrote:

"The batch of 1968 has been cruising along at high altitude as if we were immortal, and your situation has brought us down to earth. It is so easy to get caught up in the daily grind and lose the ability to distinguish between the important and the unimportant. A few of us have, for the first time, talked to our children about these issues in the past few weeks."

We discovered too the magical power of friendship and love. Our friends ministered to so many of our needs without us asking for it, or even realizing that we had these needs.

One day, while playing with Mallika, Kumar wistfully said, "I wish I could see what she will look like when she's sixteen. I'm sure she'll be very beautiful." It was hard to imagine what she would be like, for at the moment she was chubby, with a little mop of unruly curls and a huge smile.

After a while, much to our surprise, Mallika walked in dressed in a party dress of sequins and a gauzy pink scarf. Her floppy curls were scraped back and decorated with pearls and flowers. On her forehead hung the traditional oval Indian pendant studded with red and green stones. Long shiny earrings dangled on her ears and a brilliant necklace adorned her neck. She looked exactly like she would look as a teenager. A neighbour, who had overheard Kumar's remark, had taken Mallika home and dressed her up for Kumar. He was thrilled by this gesture of kindness and thoughtfulness.

We had always had a menagerie of birds when the children were young and Kumar's peacocks, turkeys, ducks and wild fowl were well known in the campus for their noise and endearing ways. The supervisor of the kitchen in the hospital had a couple of geese. Knowing Kumar's love for birds, he brought the geese and some ducks to our house every morning so that Kumar could watch them. It turned out to be more than just a therapeutic diversion, for Kumar taught Mallika to feed the geese and together they would play with the 'buck' as she called the duck. Such gestures of kindness enabled us to look forward to the next day without anxiety or worry and with a kind of happy anticipation.

One of the great sadnesses that Kumar voiced at this time was that much of our savings had gone towards his treatment and hospital admissions. "How will you manage?" he often asked. I had no real answer, except to reassure him and remind him of the many times God had provided for our needs during the past three months. Almost as an answer, Kumar's classmates from America wrote saying that they would set up a trust fund in his memory to help with the children's education.

He wept when he heard this. "Why is everyone giving me so much? What have I ever done to deserve so much love and so many blessings?"

I could only answer this question by bringing to our minds the many people to whom Kumar had given unstintingly, of his money, his time and his love, all through his life. "Cast your bread upon the waters and it shall return to you," said the wise old king in the Bible. I found it to be so true now.

We experienced a new dimension of faith. The prophet Isaiah said, "Thou wilt keep him in perfect peace whose imagination is stayed on Thee, because he trusteth in Thee." We stopped worrying about things that could happen tomorrow, and concentrated solely on all that we had for that day. In doing so we found a measure of peace.

There was a constant need to readjust our priorities and perspectives at this stage. Is it a person's achievements that give him his value? Or his status in society? Or his wealth. For us, our priority was only love. And to live for that day as if it were our last.

With acceptance came peace and a kind of happiness. The struggle was over, time for questions and the need for answers was past, it was a time for resting, and preparing for the journey ahead for both of us.

God had used physical suffering to break Kumar. With each successive relapse into coma, he changed a little. Quietly and undramatically, God filled him with a new spirit.

So many of his staff came to sit with him for a while and were heart-broken when they knew that Kumar had not much time left. Gallantly, they all put on a brave face and reminisced about the early days when they rode their cycles and bikes together along dusty roads. It did Kumar a great deal of good to know that his staff treasured the memories of those days too. Many patients also came to bid him farewell in a touching way. Some brought gifts of fruit or Kumar's favourite sweets, all of them brought memories of their own which they sat and shared with us.

Kumar was anxious to give his staff a special treat. He did not want a memorial service after his time, for people to mourn him with tears and sorrow.

"What I want is to give them all biryani (a special rice dish with meat, eaten during times of celebration) when I'm alive, and to hold a service of thanksgiving now so that I too can enjoy it with them."

So we made preparations for this unusual event. My tears flowed easily as I got ready that day. This was the last time we would ever go out as husband and wife. Kumar looked so handsome and his face glowed though there was deep sadness for him too.

"Don't cry, Ushamma, one tear from you and the staff will break down too. This service is so important to me. The focus has to be on what God has done for me, and not on what life has done to me. The glory has to go to God. Please be strong for me. Please do this for me."

I prayed for strength and peace in my heart as we walked into the little stone chapel where we had attended services all these years and where Kumar had spoken so many times. The staff had decorated the chapel in typical

Tamilian style, with crosses made out of fresh palm leaves, and with flowers and colourful leaves from the campus. The air was fragrant with the perfume of these flowers. The atmosphere, sacred. Kumar had chosen two of his favourite hymns, a prayer and a poem he wanted me to share with the staff.

Often, when Kumar was too tired to read, I would read aloud significant poems and passages to him. The poem he had chosen for today, was from a book he had ordered for me a year earlier, and yet reached my hands only a few days ago. I marvelled at the timing of it. The poem by Amy Carmichael seemed as if it was written especially for him, as it was exactly what Kumar felt.

"Before the winds that blow do cease,
Teach me to dwell within Thy calm:
Before the pain has passed in peace,
Give me my God, to sing a psalm.
Let me not loose the chance to prove
The fullness of enabling love.
O love of God, do this for me:
Maintain a constant victory.

Before I leave the desert land
For meadows of immortal flowers,
Lead me where streams at Thy command
Flow by the borders of the hours,
That when the thirsty come, I may
Show them the fountains in the way,
O tow of God, do this for me:,
Maintain a constant victory."

The lunch after the service was a celebration under the trees in Karigiri style. Long, wooden benches laid with banana leaves, glasses of cold water, and a laddu (a sweet dessert served at special times) also made it a festive occasion. Kumar had invited all the staff who were now working at Karigiri, about three hundred and fifty people, and some who had retired a few years earlier, as well as a few of his old, beloved patients.

Everybody was amazed at Kumar's inner strength and the radiance that flowed out of him. Many ate with tears flowing into their food. Kumar was in good spirits, enjoying the biryani and joking with everyone. The staff could see that Kumar was at peace, that he had accepted that this was God's Will for him, and that this day was a gift of gratitude to God, and a plea to maintain a constant victory through everything.

God was giving Kumar little glimpses of how the children would look like and be as teenagers. One night after our family prayers, John-John hugged Kumar and said, "Appa, when I grow up I am going to be a liver surgeon and every time I operate on someone, I will think of you." Kumar was so moved. Not just by John's feelings, and his thoughts of the future, but because he knew that this desire was planted by God and that John too would one day follow his vision, just like he himself had done so many years ago. Thus was he reassured of his little son's future.

Kumar had seen Jamie change from a happy-go-lucky boy, to one who was caring, responsible, always loving and supportive to his parents. From his own experience, he knew the difficulties and responsibilities that faced a young boy without a father.

During the last few years he had tried to teach the boys the many things that he loved passionately. He taught them to fish, to enjoy long walks and climb hills. He even taught them to hunt and shoot, to skin rabbits and cook on an open fire. Loud rock music was another great passion which he shared with them enthusiastically. Although he was an indulgent fun-loving father, he also insisted on their obeying him from the time they were very little.

There was a group of monkeys which terrorized the patients and families on the campus. One of these monkeys came inside our house and frightened Mallika. Kumar asked for his gun, and walking with great difficulty, went out and shot one of the monkeys. Exhausted by this action, he gave the gun back to Jamie to unload.

Suddenly, he found a much larger monkey lunging towards him viciously. "Reload and fire, quickly, Jamie" he said. Jamie obeyed him and shot the second monkey dead just a few feet away from Kumar. Kumar was so amazed at Jamie's quick reflexes and his obedience. "I'm so proud of you, my son," he told Jamie. "You've learnt all that I taught you well. I'm so proud of you." He was at peace knowing that Jamie had learnt some of the lessons he had tried to teach him.

As he became weaker, spending time with the boys, preparing them for his end, now became a priority. The boys were losing their beloved father and it was a frightening time for them. They were beside him all the time, laughing with him, holding on to him, loving him in every way they could. At intervals they would go into the bathroom and cry their hearts out, and emerge a few moments later, red-eyed, but composed, and with a smile on their faces for their father. In spite of being so incapacitated, Kumar realized that he could still do things for them to show them how much he loved them, things that may be important to them in the years ahead. He told them stories of when he was young, and shared so many parts of his early life with them. He told them the legend of the buried Jesudasan treasure, which his father had told him when he was a little boy, and whet their appetite for adventure. He was honest with them about the many mistakes he had made and hoped that they wouldn't make the same ones too. He told them about the silly things that he had done, of all the things which had brought him immense happiness and gave them little fatherly tips on growing up. He held them close to him all the time, and constantly kissed and cuddled them and told them funny jokes, so that their time with him was full of laughter.

At the start of the illness, Jamie once told him, "Appa, if you die, I can never believe in God, not after all the prayers we've said, not after seeing you suffer so much."

Because Jamie and John-John were so young, he was most concerned that they should not let this tragedy undermine their faith. He wanted to pass on his faith, his trust and the need for obedience to God, that he had learned over the years, in a way that they would understand.

His arms around them, his head on their shoulders, he would say, "I love you Jamie son, I love you John-

John. I know you will miss me, I will miss you too. But don't forget that we will be together one day. Appa will always be near you, only you won't be able to see me. Have faith. There will be times when you will question God, just like I did, and be angry, and that's natural. He wants us to be open and honest and share our feelings with Him. He knows how we feel because Jesus too has been through pain and suffering and knows what it is to be lonely. Don't let my illness and death cut you off from God, so that you don't want to be with Him, listen to Him, or speak to Him. That would be a tragedy."

"Much in life is not fair, I think you know all about that. The point about my illness is not why it happened, but all that we learned from it. How God provided for all of our needs, gave us strength, brought me to this point of healing and acceptance so that I can die in peace. You know the story of Job who lost everything and was struck by disease. Like him, I too have come to the point where I can say, 'Even though You slay me, yet will I trust in Thee.'

"I won't be with you to take you through the rest of your life. I want you to think, as you grow up, about what you will do with all that you have been through with me. The pain, the sadness, is not to be wasted. Will you close your mind and heart to suffering? Will you walk away when you see someone in need or in pain? Or will you be open and help someone, sharing what you have learned, knowing what we have been through, bringing comfort and hope to those who need it?"

"I can tell you for certain now that God has taken this terrible disease, and my pain and dying, and will make something good come out of it in the end. You may not see this now, or for a long while yet, but one day you will, and you will be thankful that it all happened as it did."

"He has a plan for each of your lives, just as He had for mine. You will have to ask Him for guidance to show you the way and live up to what He sets before you. The greatest joy comes from doing His Will and knowing that you are truly loved by Him. You are wonderful boys. So many times I've yelled at you and been unfair to you, but you have always been forgiving because you love me so much. That's how God loves and forgives you too. So never feel ashamed to ask Him to forgive you when you do something wrong. The devil will try his best to make you lose your faith, but hold on during these times to my faith. This legacy of faith is all that I'm leaving you, that and all my love."

In acceptance lies peace. Kumar had found this to be true after such a long time. To remain in peace also meant that he had to clean out parts of his life that still caused him distress.

Thus started a period of reconciliation.

For a while, he had fallen out with a close friend. The night of the service in the garden, Kumar called for her. "Will you visit? I'd like to see you," he said. I was surprised as I knew how much they had hurt each other. "Will you bring me something to eat that you have cooked?" he asked. It was good to see the two friends sitting in the garden the next day laughing and enjoying each other's company again. The pain and resentment of a strained relationship had just melted away for both of them. Yet, I knew that now there was a different kind of pain for them to endure, for their hearts were pierced with the sorrow of Kumar's impending end and the grief of loss.

We learned from this experience too that a relationship that is complete in friendship need never end, for there is nothing left unsaid, or undone. When a dying person and a loved one come to feel complete and 'as one' between themselves, the feelings are of joy and deep affection, as well as the inevitable sadness.

Similarly, Kumar called many of the staff whom he had hurt during his years at work, some who felt that he had been unfair or hard on them, and asked them to forgive him. He gave away many of his things to those who had served him faithfully over the years.

The final test came when a previous Director, who had caused him a lot of grief at one point, visited. For many years, there had been bitter and angry feelings between them. Now hearing about Kumar's illness, he had come to see him, and was shocked at the change in Kumar. Gone was the strong, challenging, arrogant personality. To his sadness, he found a frail, gentle Kumar, still challenging, but in a different way. He brought his good wishes and blessings for Kumar. Kumar held his hands and gracefully accepted them, and in his inimitable way broke the tension between them with one of his jokes. In that moment, all the old animosity vanished with the laughter. There was peace between them as the two men chatted like old friends. They parted finally with the firm knowledge that the years of mistrust and misunderstandings were over, and that both of them had forgiven each other. Thus was peace restored between them.

The family was stunned at this turn of events. So was the community watching us. "How could you sit there and hold his hand as if nothing happened?" many people asked Kumar.

In reply Kumar explained, "All that grieves and hurts, all the fights, the manipulations, the desire to have things one's own way, the need to be right, are all only for a moment. So too is all that pleases us and makes us happy. In the final tally, the only things that really matter are the things which will last till eternity. We cause so much grief to each other in petty ways because of ambition, pride and greed. We want the applause, the credits, the awards for ourselves. There comes a time, like this time for me, when I realize that all that matters is not power or fame, but the love one has given and received. That is all I want to remember now, nothing else matters. And I am grateful that there has been so much love in my life."

One day, Kumar held me in his arms and said, "What's on your mind, Ushamma?"

I was afraid of the next coma as I knew that that would be the end. "How will I say goodbye to you? How will I be able to watch those first coma signs and not do anything at all?" I cried.

There was a hard ball of coldness and fear which I had been carrying around inside my stomach for days now. Kumar understood these fears, and knew that he couldn't let me face it all alone. So many times before, we had sat down and worked out a strategy for the things that had worried us. Now we had to do it again, but this time there was a big difference. I was to face it all on my own.

Kumar asked me to get my Bible and together we re-read all the passages that dealt with fear.

When fear strikes and we are afraid, we are told to "Be still" and to rest in the presence of God. We are to come into His presence with the sure knowledge that He is God. That He is in control of everything. That He is aware of all that is happening to us.

I recorded in my diary that, "He knows exactly how I'm feeling. How alone, and sad and worn out. He knows too exactly what is going to happen to Kumar, to me and the children. He knows the causes of my fear and my confusion and He's there for me in all this too."

The Bible tells us to : *"Rest in Him.*
To cease striving.
For He knows our needs."

"I will not leave you nor forsake you," is the great Bible promise. This was what I truly needed to believe, with every cell in my body. That no matter what, I would not have to face anything on my own. As He was with me before, during the early days of the coma and the stay in the ICU, so He would be with me now too, during the times I dreaded most, of seeing Kumar slip into a final coma. He would be with me even when it was all over and there was nothing left but grief.

Once we are still and quiet in His presence we are to seek His guidance about what to do next. He will surely lead and guide.

"Do not be afraid, for I am with you, even unto the end of the world," said Jesus.

These sentences, written down in my diary, gave us both strength and courage to face the days ahead. We read these words written by Old Testament stalwarts like Jacob, Moses, Joshua and David. We read them again and again until they seeped into us and became part of our bloodstream and our thinking.

Our best times were out in the garden sitting in the sun, watching the children at play. Kumar had a very special relationship with my mother, and wanted to be with her during his last days. Holding her hand, he would remind her of the days when he first came into our family. "I have to confess something now, Mum," he said sheepishly. "Do you remember that first Christmas I was in England and you baked a beautiful cake and left it on the refrigerator? Well, I came down early and opened the fridge and the cake fell down and broke. I was miserable. Anyway, I put it back in exactly the same place knowing that the same thing would happen to the next person who opened the fridge. And that of course was you. You were equally upset with yourself." They laughed so much at this memory, and of many more since then.

Then he reminded Mum of all the embarrassing things I did when I first came to Karigiri as a new bride. The morning would be spent in laughter or in deep thought and reflection.

This was also a time for sheer indulgence. I removed all his previous dietary restrictions and made special dishes for him. It was like being newly married all over again. Those early days, I would try out various new recipes, set the table beautifully with decorative napkins and flowers, and surprise Kumar. Now, after all these years, I was doing it again. His eyes would light up at the sight of a souffle, or Chinese soup, or tandoori chicken. His tray would have a crystal vase with a single rose from our garden. Again it brought back memories of being a new bride, for this is how Kumar used to wake me up in the mornings those days—with a cup of coffee.

Bath time too, was a special treat for both of us and a time of great fun and joy. I had bought some aromatic oils, and a friend gave a bottle of bubble bath for Kumar to enjoy. The idea was not just to give him a bath that would make him clean, but to prolong the time so that we could have fun splashing each other, caressing each other and watch the glistening bubbles glide down each other's skin. The warmth, the exotic fragrances and the almost erotic nature of the frivolousness, made it a special time for both of us.

Being at home all the time tested Kumar's patience sorely. "Take me for a drive," he pleaded one day. So we did. We drove around the hill to our old picnic haunts. We stopped at the lake for a while and watched the birds. The sun was just going down and the sky was streaked with orange and pink. "I'm sure heaven will be an even more beautiful place," he said, looking at the sky.

No amount of acceptance however diminishes the dreadful reality of suffering. The nausea made it so difficult for him to eat anything, though his appetite was quite good and he was often hungry. The pain still ripped him apart on occasions. His walk too had gradually deteriorated till it was painful and slow, for he found it difficult to pick up his swollen feet. Finally he needed the help of a walking stick. "The final blow to my ego!" he called it.

Kumar's thoughts constantly returned to the process of dying. 'What will it really be like? Will it hurt? Will I know what's happening?" In spite of our own openness, even his medical friends were unwilling to talk about his impending death or discuss it with him. So I read up as much as I could about it and shared it all with him.

The fear of the physical process of dying was removed finally by a passage from Steven Levine's *Who Dies?* In it, the author explains the experience of dying based on the ancient concepts of the body being composed of elements of earth, water, fire and air. He writes that as death approaches, the earth element, that is the hardness and solidity of the body, begins to melt . As it melts, boundaries and edges we know it begin to break into a fine state of fluidity. This gives way to the fluid movements of the water element. Then the fire element takes over and the experience is of warm mist. This is the time when body functions like circulation and respiration slow down. The mist offers a lightness of being, and finally the air element takes over and the mistiness dissolves into pure being. No pain, no stress, all competely natural. The body is left behind, while the pure being, the soul, soars.

Kumar could never remember what happened while he was in a coma. Because I told him so, he knew that he was in no pain, or discomfort. He could feel neither cold nor heat. So he was able to identify with this passage and the gentle and natural way in which the process of dying was described.

An ancient prayer by Francis de Sales, became his own.

"One day my soul must depart from this body.
When will it be?
In winter or in summer?
In town or in country?
During the day or the night?
Suddenly or with warning?
Due to illness or an accident?
Shall I have a chance to confess my sins?
Shall there be a priest to assist me?
I know none of these things.
One thing only is certain that I will die,
and sooner than I would like.
Dear God, take me into your arms on that special day.
Set my whole heart on your promise of heaven.
Guide my feet in your ways O Lord,
That I may walk the straight path to eternal life.
Let me cast off everything that holds me back
on my journey there,
So that all of my strengths may be directed
towards that goal."

Kumar knew that he would not be alone, and that I would be beside him, holding him, loving him until the end. But he was fearful of being alone after his soul had left his body.

We found a poem by Amy Carmichael, *Carried by Angels* which spoke to him deeply and brought a measure of peace and comfort to know that he would not be alone either while he was dying or after that too.

> "It is all we know of how they go;
> The angels carry them;
> The way they know.
> Our kind Lord told us so."

One morning as he woke up, he snuggled into my shoulder, whispering, "I love you, Ushamma." I was still half asleep, but I liked what I heard. "I can see a cross, Ushamma," he said.

I dozed off and woke up with a start a few minutes later, as I had to get breakfast for the boys and Kumar. Giving him a quick kiss, I said I'd be back in ten minutes. When I returned he was still asleep, so I put his head back on my shoulder and cuddled him. His head felt unusually heavy, and his eyes were glazed. With a shock, I realized he had slipped into a coma again. This was for the fourth time.

Sitting there, holding his hand, I realized that the terrible fear that I had anticipated with the oncoming of a final coma had dissolved. I was calm as I remembered the words of all that we had read and prepared together, and knew exactly what I had to do. We made him comfortable and according to his wishes kept him on our bed. I began the long vigil at his bedside.

The boys were heart-broken and in great despair, but they knew that this was how Kumar wanted it, as he had spoken to them and prepared them for it.

As we sat by his bedside, I read the passage from the Bible that he had asked me to read for Jamie and John-John when he went into a final coma.

"Do not let your hearts be troubled. Trust in God, trust also in me. In my Father's house are many rooms; if it were not so l would have told you. I am going there to prepare a place for you, I will come back and take you to be with me that you may also be where I am going." (John 14:1-4)

Our families and friends were shocked and upset that I was keeping Kumar at home and not taking him to hospital for treatment. Dying at home, facing the end positively without medical interventions, and having one's own family take care of you during the process of dying, were all unusual in that no one in our family or community had done it this way before. They found it difficult to accept that this was Kumar's wish. Many people had thought that I was humouring Kumar when I agreed to allow him to die at home. But when they realized that I meant to honour my promise to him, they were very angry with me.

A lot of pressure was put on me to take him to hospital. An old colleague from Karigiri threatened to take me to court if I didn't take Kumar to hospital within the hour. Friends from the town of Ambur drove all the way up saying, "If you don't want him alive, we do," and planned on taking him to hospital themselves. The children and I had to stand against our bedroom door, to prevent them from taking Kumar away. Aunts of mine who came from Madras said, "God heals through medicines and doctors and you are doing wrong by denying him that." My Dad too was very angry with me. "He cannot decide something like this for himself, he is not in a fit state mentally to make such a decision. You should do what is best for him."

My own heart was breaking saying goodbye to Kumar and here were so many well-meaning people harassing me and saying things which broke my heart further. I remembered the passages on fear that I had written down. There, sitting on our bed beside Kumar, I made a little place for myself in silence, and in calmness came before the presence of God. I sat still, knowing He was God, and in full control of everything. He knew the unfair accusations that were hurled at me and my pain, I knew that He would see me through it all. When I was sure of this, and when I felt His Peace in my heart, I asked for His guidance and asked Him to lead me through the difficult days ahead.

A whole day passed, and by the next morning, there were more agonies to face.

Many of Kumar's medical friends from the Christian Medical College were angry that I was not giving him insulin for his diabetes or even water on a drip. "Life should be prolonged for as long as we can. How can you do this to him? How could you want him to die? Think of the children. How could you put them through all this?"

More and more unjust reproaches were thrown at me. There was anger too at the use of mild sedation for pain and restlessness.

Dr George Kurian was also under a lot of pressure from the medical community and friends. Unable to bear it any more and wanting to do the right thing, he finally asked me whether I should think about whether we should give Kumar insulin for his diabetes. Kumar had been very particular that nothing should be given to him when he went into a final coma. No insulin, no drips, no fluids. Only mild sedation for pain and restlessness, so that he could die in peace and dignity.

"George, how can I go back on my promise to him? He trusted me to take care of everything for him the way he wanted it. I have never let him down so far. How can I let him down now when he needs me the most?" The anguish was causing me a great deal of pain, but I knew for certain that the trust and love on which our marriage had been built and which bound him to me, especially at this time, could not now be broken.

The boys were very distressed at the comments, and the way people harassed me. But they understood and respected my promise to Kumar. They were very supportive.

Jamie hugged me and said, "Do what you have to do for Appa, Amma. This is what Appa wanted, he loved you and trusted you to do this for him. You know we love you. Don't worry about what anyone else says."

I sat outside on the verandah where I had sat so many times before during times of despair and hopelessness. A cool breeze was blowing gently. The lush greens and bright yellows in the garden helped to bring a sense of tranquility to my anguished heart as I prayed for guidance. "Lord, I can't take this anymore. Please help. Give me your strength and patience. Help me to understand that everyone loves Kumar so much that they are as broken as I am and do not know how to react. Help me not to hurt anyone or retaliate in anger." There was a commotion at the door and I raised my head to see what it was about.

Jamie was standing beside me. There was something quite odd about what was happening and it took me a few minutes to figure out what it was. Jamie had a broad smile on his face. Gone was the tense look of despair that I had seen on him for so long. "Come on Amma, Appa is awake, he's calling for you."

I couldn't believe what I heard. As I went into our room, I saw Kumar, sitting up in bed, smiling, holding out his arms for me. George sat by the foot of the bed stunned. "It just cannot happen this way," he kept saying. Kumar looked calm and fresh, though very weak. There was none of the trauma of waking up in confusion or anger or restlessness, as in the ICU. In fact he was back to his usual jovial self. Seeing George's look of amazement he said, "Fooled you, didn't I?"

Like us, Kumar also accepted that this was a strange miracle. Would this miracle finally bring the healing we had all prayed for? Sadly, no. Then what was the point of it? Why would something that was supposed to be medically impossible happen this way?

I think it was God's way of telling the medical community, which was arrogant in thinking that modern medical interventions and drugs sustained life, that Kumar's life was in His hands and that his end depended on His timing. Not on antibiotics, anti-coma regimen and ICU procedures.

News of Kumar's miraculous awakening spread quickly and everybody rejoiced with us. Dr Anand Zachariah cycled all the seventeen kilometres to Karigiri that night to see Kumar and to ask if there was anything he needed.

Kumar asked him, "What happened to me, Anand, what next?"

Sitting beside Kumar, holding his hands, his eyes moist, Anand replied' "I don't know, Kumar. There are no medical explanations for what happened to you. I don't know what tomorrow will be like. We will still take it one day at a time."

Kumar could not remember anything of what had happened while he was in coma. He could not remember saying, "I can see a cross." He was delighted when I told him about it.

"I know for certain now that the cross, and the resurrection, is true. I believe that Jesus is real and is waiting for me. God in his mercy and love has taken away the fear of death from me after this coma. The revelation of the cross just before I went into the coma is His final assurance to me that I will be in His hands. The sureness of knowing that God will be near me at the moment of dying, the promise of a wonderful eternal life, with no more pain or suffering makes the journey through the valley of the shadow of Death no longer dark and frightening."

The missionary Amy Carmichael said,

"The call to enter for the second time into any painful experience is a sign of our Lord's confidence. It offers a great opportunity."

Kumar had been through these painful coma experiences four times and certainly there had been the opportunity. To be a witness. To live out his faith. To live trusting and obeying his God.

The days that followed were particularly traumatic for me. Kumar's brother and several members of my family could not still accept that Kumar was so ill. They tried to persuade me to have another opinion from another hospital, another specialist, convinced that someone else would come up with a magical cure. There was great pressure to try alternative medical practices in search of a cure. There were many angry calls, and hurtful visitors to face. "Help me to stay calm, help me not to retaliate in anger, help me to forgive those who don't understand," was my constant prayer.

Kumar wrote out a Living Will, to be used in the event of further harassment during the next coma. He spoke to his brother and sister about how important dying in dignity was for him, of how much pain he had suffered over the years. He wanted them to understand that he did not want to die, that he was not giving up. He wanted very much to live, but if that was not posiible, then he wanted their support in dying well. He wanted to spare the children and me the agony of seeing him suffer while he was dying. He repeatedly asked George to be with me at home when he went into the final coma, and was reassured only when all of us said that we would respect his wishes and allow him to go in peace and dignity.

In spite of such difficulties, the days that followed were special and full of tenderness and love for us. Kumar sat outside in the garden with flowers in a dozen shades of yellow around him, his Bible open on his lap, his eyes often turned heavenwards. We knew that he could slip away again at any time, so every second we had together was precious. Kumar couldn't bear to have me leave his side for even a minute. At the same time, there were times when he needed to be "alone" with just his thoughts. He had to separate himself from all that he loved in order to be able to leave in peace. It was not a time of rejection, but a period of serious reflection, when he mentally "surrendered" all that once captivated and held him to this world. Although I understood this need, it was especially hard for me to bear.

Kumar was most particular now that his end should be significant to others as well. Just as we had once carefully chosen the readings and hymns for our wedding service, he now chose the readings and prayers for his funeral service. He made me bring out all my poetry books and special books. I read so many things out aloud. He was very particular that every reading at his funeral should focus on the glory of God.

"The service could so easily turn into a melodrama of weeping and wailing. I want it to be a service of thanksgiving and praise."

He was ready to face his Lord. Having said all his goodbyes, having done all that he wanted to do, he now waited eagerly for the end. Charles Spurgeon in a sermon, said, *"We are immortal until our work is done."* Kumar felt that all his work was now done. He had even found a place for us to live, after he was gone.

Kumar was always one for giving gifts. Now so near the end, there were still some gifts left for him to give. He sat at the computer one day, putting in silly jokes for me to read after he was gone. "Who will make you laugh once I'm gone?" he said. He knew that losing him would be hard for us all to bear. He knew that for the children, and for John-John especially, that there could be permanent scars. So he wanted to make his death a gift for us, a time when we would remember not only the sadness, but also the dignity, the peace and the courage with which he faced his end.

Expressions of love and gratitude flowed from him to everybody. He spoke to the children of dying in peace, without bitterness or anger that this had happened to him. "Always remember the love we have all had from so many people all through this time. And think of this time as the best time of our lives, because it really is."

One day, after reading his Bible, he said, "I've written some things for you, Ushamma, I want you to read them after I'm gone. I will leave it here in your Bible for you. It's a gift from me to you."

He believed with all his heart that God would not make a mistake in transferring him from earth to heaven and when it happened, he knew that the timing would be perfect. The awakening from the coma made him feel that going to heaven was like passing from one room to another and nothing to be afraid of.

He shared his thoughts with those who were close to him. "At times God puts us through a period of darkness or pain, to teach us to look up to Him, to be quiet before Him and to listen to Him. Even if we have had wonderful faith, there comes a point in our lives when we are against the wall, when everything we know for sure, begins to break up and slowly disappear. That's when we need to say, I am in darkness and pain, Lord, teach me to be quiet and listen to you. Teach me to trust you. To me, when it seemed that God had abandoned me, when everything that I held on to had crumbled, when there was nothing else left to cling to, I finally found my way back to God again. I thought he had deserted me, but I realized that he had never really gone away, but was there always like the father of the prodigal son. Waiting. Watching. Hoping. All He was asking of me was that I trust Him and accept the painful pruning that would eventually bring me to a new life."

Every night was a time for rejoicing and thanking God for one more day. It was also a time for saying a final goodbye in case he never woke up again. He truly believed, as the familiar hymn says,

"Green Pastures are before me,
Which yet I have not seen,
Bright skies will soon be over me,
Where the dark clouds have been.
My hope I cannot measure,
My path to life is free,
My Saviour has my treasure,
And He will walk with me."

Jamie, John-John and Mallika were his treasures, and he knew they were in safe hands. The boys would cuddle up against Kumar, we would have a reading from the Bible, prayers, some jokes and they would kiss him good night.

On this particular night, the Zachariahs had brought us a meaningful book of poems by Joe Mannath. There was a section entitled *Facing My Death*.

"Read it out for me," said Kumar.
"1 believe
that you will call me
When it is best for me.
I believe
that your love has prepared for me
joys beyond my grasp.
My strength fails
my cleverness is of no avail;
My loved ones cannot come with me,
You alone -
You will be there at my side,
as you have always been,
You will hold me,
guide me,
receive me,
and remake my broken frame.
In your name I surrender
the remaining hours of my life,
knowing that the best is yet to come."

"This is written just for me, isn't it?" he said, and then to break up the tenseness of the moment, he pulled the children over for another big hug.
"See you in the morning, Appa," they said, with hope.
"See you in the morning, son," he replied with a kiss.
They lingered on for one more cuddle, one more kiss.

Early on the morning of 19th February, Kumar slipped into a fifth coma.

Once more, we began a period of waiting, not on anyone or anything, but on God--for strength, for peace in our hearts and for wisdom. John-John was heart-broken as he lay on Kumar's bed in the verandah, wrapped up in his blanket, silent tears pouring down his face. I sat with him for a while, our tears mingling.

He held me tight and prayed, "Please God, give Appa a peaceful end, don't let him suffer anymore." This simple prayer was wrung out of his grieving heart. All I could do was thank God that he had given this little child His grace and love to pray for what was best for his father, despite his own pain. Jamie was strong enough to sit with Kumar and hold his hand. "Please God, be with Appa and hear our prayers for him. Give him a peaceful end." This was my prayer too.

Aunty and Uncle Zachariah came to stay with us during this difficult period, providing the care and love we so badly needed. Every night, Kumar's doctor friends from Christian Medical College would take turns to come and spend the night with us as they did not want me to be alone in case Kumar, died during the night. So they came and sat beside him, caring for him and being with me, giving me the strength and love which I so badly needed at that time. Their presence was a great source of support as close family members were unable to just stand by and do nothing but wait. To the medical profession, death is a failure, yet to us, who had accepted all thls, death was to be a release, an answer to our prayer, the doorway to a new life.

For four days, we watched over Kumar. I removed the heavy winter curtains and replaced them with white, lacy ones, which allowed shafts of sunlight to seep through. The room was filled with fresh flowers. Kumar lay on soft sheets, and was covered with his favourite blanket. The music, which he loved, played softly in the background. Beside him were those whom he loved and who loved him dearly.

To discourage visitors from coming home and yet to allow them to share in our pain, the boys had put up a notice on our gate which said, "Please pray for us." It was most touching to see the staff and patients drop to their knees in front of our house, and turn their eyes towards heaven.

Despite the sadness and the grief, we were wrapped in such love. Kumar's decision to allow us to care for him at home, to change him, to see that he was kept fresh and clean, and to have all his personal needs attended to, was not just a matter of trust. It was his final gift to us. For caring in this way, and being cared for, is a powerful, final expression of love.

Although he was not aware of it, little acts like wiping his forehead with a cold cloth, massaging his legs, keeping his lips moist, turning him over so that he did not develop sores, were meaningful ways for us to show him that he was still precious to us. That we loved him. That it was a privilege, and not a burden for us to care for him. He lay there, quietly accepting all the love that was poured out of everyone's hearts for him. By caring for him in this unusual way, we had created a small community amongst ourselves, and had got closer to one another. The dignity in his dying lay not in outward appearances, or in his position, but in his courage, his personal integrity, and the love with which many of his actions were motivated throughout his life, and the positive way in which he faced his death.

Kumar lay quietly, his pulse steadily dropping. It was time to say goodbye.

"Speak peace to my soul, O Lord," I prayed as I sat beside Kumar. After a while Uncle Zac asked me to sleep as he felt I needed the rest to be able to cope later on. Reluctantly, I lay in our guest room after lunch.

Just as I was drifting off to sleep, I thought I heard Kumar's laugh. It was a pleasant dream. The laugh echoed again and again. So clearly. I sat up confused. It wasn't a dream. I went back to our bedroom and slowly opened the door. There was Kumar sitting up in bed, talking to Aunty Zac, asking her to read some poetry for him.

At first, I didn't understand what was happening and was a little disturbed to see Kumar propped up against the pillows. As I neared the bed, I could see that he was awake and smiling. He held his arms out to me--and I sank into them.

It took a few moments for it to sink into me, that Kumar was awake again.After four days of being in a coma, with no fluids or medicines, he was awake again and normal. Another miracle!

He was so amazed that he had been in a coma for so many days. "I'm hungry, Ushamma, will you make me some porridge?" I asked someone to make it for him as I couldn't bear to leave him.

"No, I want you to make it, only you know just how I like it." The jokes were all back though he was very weak. Looking around he was pleased that l had kept my promises to him about having fresh flowers and candles in the room.

"Where did you get these mangy looking flowers from, Ushamma?" he teased me.

There was time again for a few more hours of precious conversation. Lots more kisses and one last prayer together. "See you in the morning darling, I love you." he said, as he drifted off to sleep.

There was no morning, in the way we had expected, as sometime during the night he had two internal bleeds and had slipped back into a deep coma. This was for the sixth time. The waiting began again, saying our goodbyes, surrounding him with love.

On the morning of the 24th of February, Kumar's pulse started to drop, and his breathing became slower. People imagine that an unconscious person who is dying, cannot see or hear or feel anything, and at this stage there is nothing that can be done for them. I was convinced that despite the coma, Kumar could still hear me. I held his hand and bending close to his ear reassured him that I was still beside him, that I loved him with all my heart and that I would miss him so much. I thanked him for all the happy years he had given me, for all the beautiful things he had bought me, for all the laughter and the fun being his wife was. It was his wish that I sing the 23rd Psalm for him as he left our world and went into the new one with his Lord.

Dr Fritschi and his wife, Aunty Mano, had joined us and a last morsel of bread and drop of wine was put on his lip. Each of us read a favourite psalm or passage from the Bible, that was meaningful to us, for him. We sang hymns that came alive for us with promise and meaning.

"Hold Thou Thy cross before my closing eyes,

Shine through the gloom and point me to the skies.

Heaven's morning breaks and earth's vain shadows flee,

In life in death, O Lord, abide with me."

So much of our life flashed past me. Kumar slipping a ring on my finger for the first time. Kumar rocking the boys to sleep. Kumar jogging, his feet pounding on the Karigiri highway, Kumar playing with Mallika, the long walks at sunset, the warm caresses and passionate moments of loving each other in spite of so much sadness. So much was being lost.

Just as Kumar was dying, I too seemed to be dying inside me. Would there ever be a springtime in my life, I wondered, as I sat there with my head against his heart. It was the hardest, longest, most tedious time of my life. A time of silence, a time of clinging, and yet, a time of letting go. I could feel the Spirit of God all around me. Our bedroom was no longer our bedroom, it had become a sacred place, a place where the presence of God could be felt day and night. There was love in the faces of all those close to us. Love for Kumar but also for us his family. Every person there had the strength and the love to sit beside him without the fear and revulsion that death normally brings.

Dr George Kurian, sitting beside his friend and patient, whispered words of farewell. "Go in peace, friend, go in peace." Uncle and Aunty Zacharaiah caressed his hands and his face so tenderly. Jamie sitting beside his father, red-eyed and broken, whispered, "I love you, Appa, go in peace Appa."

The grief after a while, gave way to thankfulness as I remembered so many blessing of friends and family and the many ways in which God had provided for all of our needs and granted every desire of Kumar's throughout his life. Even to the extent of blessing him with a beautiful, beloved daughter in a most unexpected manner. This was no time really for mourning, as God was answering our prayers for a peaceful end for Kumar. Those whom he loved the most were beside him, loving him, whispering messages of love and farewell, as he journeyed nearer and nearer towards the other side.

"Go in peace, sweetheart," I said, and kissed his forehead. One last quiet sigh and Kumar's soul was carried away by the angels sent to bring him home.

Dr Fritschi prayed,

"Go forth, O Christian soul,
In the name of the Father who created you,
In thee name of the Son who redeems you,
And in the name of the Holy Spirit who carries you
Into the bosom of the Father."

Kumar was dead. So many feelings washed over me... sadness at the loss, fear of loneliness and all the changes his death would bring, despair when I thought of the children, and yet even at this time, there was thankfulness for a peaceful end, and a sense of victory and joy. The months of pain and suffering were at last over. Death did not drag him away, or crush him in its vice-like grip, nor did it overpower him with fear and darkness. Like many of the faithful down the ages, Kumar too overcame death by facing it with dignity, courage and the complete faith that he was going to his Lord's presence. so I could honestly ask, "Where O death is thy sting?" Far from being something to shrink from, or to fear, Kumar's death had been a positive, blessed experience for all who were around him.

Then, reality hit me that he was gone forever. My tears flowed as I looked at him and held him in my arms one last time.

The bitter news of Kumar's death spread all over the campus within minutes. Staff and so many of his old patients lined up outside our house, quietly singing the 23rd Psalm in Tamil. They walked past him weeping, touching his feet, singing his favourite Tamil hymns. The dignity of his death, the courage which he displayed throughout his illness, the faith that he put on view all through his life and the distinction and quality of the life that he lived, had flowed into all those who came to pay their final respects to him.

The funeral was to be one of praise and thanksgiving, not one of morbid grieving, and Kumar, in his meticulous way, had seen to that by choosing the readings and the people he wanted to read them. The tiny chapel at Karigiri looked beautiful with dozens of white flowers. The scent of rose, jasmine and lilies mingled to produce a lovely fragrance. Hundreds of patients huddled together outside, looking lost in their grief. The cortege passed slowly by the Department of Epidemiology one last time as staff paid their respects to him with a silent prayer.

Dr Anand Zachariah, his beloved physician of many years, read:

Do not stand at my grave and weep,
I am not there. I do not sleep......
Do not stand at my grave and cry.
I am not there.
I did not die.

Perhaps, this brought a measure of comfort to those who mourned him, as they filed past his body, paying their last respects.

Those who mourned the most were his patients who came from every corner of Gudiyathum taluk. He had served them well and cared for them lovingly for twenty-one years. Now he was gone, their loss was irreplaceable. They came on crutches, on feet that were just stumps. They limped, dragging one foot behind the other. Some were carried, the blind were led, the elderly plodded slowly.

Mounds of flowers were laid on him. So many hearts were full of loss and the specialness of the service ministered to them all.

People of all faiths had prayed for healing for Kumar; now with his death, for many, their faith was shaken, and Kumar wanted to give it back to them. "Don't grieve," he wanted to say to them, "Praise Him instead, for great is

His faithfulness." He had chosen a song that had been a theme song throughout his life.

"This is my story, this is my song,
Praising my Saviour all the day long."

Thus was Kumar laid to rest in a quiet spot near the chapel at Karigiri, under the spreading branches of a beautiful rain tree.

14. Epilogue

Kumar's death cut deeply into our lives and we experienced pain, sadness and an immeasurable sense of loss. The pattern of our lives changed and the harmony in our family life was shattered. For much of the time, I felt that I was living in an emotional wilderness. There were days when I felt strong enough to face the future alone, and there were days when I just could not get out of bed. There were days when I wanted to keep every single thing, and there were days when I went into an orgy of destruction. Peace and anguish seemed to exist side by side within me.

Letters and cards of condolence arrived from every part of the world. While it was good to know that so many people cared about Kumar and would miss him, it also made the reality of his death more painful. Kumar had passed safely through the Valley of the Shadow of Death on to the other side. He was at peace, in a place which for him was now home. For me, there was grief, tears and an inconsolable sense of loss. My 'home' was gone.

The reality of being without him kept hitting me from every angle. Being alone in the evenings, waking up alone, going for a walk alone, seeing his empty place at the table, all proved to be too much to handle, and there were days when I could do nothing except sit on my verandah and gaze at all my flowers.

One night after the children had gone to bed, all I felt was abject total loss. I re-read my diary, again and again, remembering Kumar's words, his feelings, and all the pain. It was the first time I had been alone since Kumar died. The grace and strength that had been with me during Kumar's last days seemed to have disappeared, and all I could feel was darkness and despair. I longed for light, for guidance, for companionship and for love in my life again. Almost out of habit and a desperate need, I picked up my Bible. As I opened it I found the 'gifts' Kumar had left for me and asked me to read after he was gone.

"My darling Ushamma,
Your radiance is like the rising sun,
Your beauty lights up the world,
You wear the sun and moon as your jewels
(so you don't need any more!)
Your eyes are like a lotus petal,
(so you don't need any make-up)
Your face is fragrant like champaka
(so there go your perfumes!)
Your hair is like incense.
My Ushamma,
She has capacities.....use them!
She is active,
She is aware,
She is fearless,
She is free!"

I knew that there were a few more of these and decided to read the others on days when I felt miserably low.

"I love my wife with wonder and adoration,
Cannot believe God's love for me
In getting her to me for eternity.
Wonderful times we've had and enjoyed
Love and making love.
Tenderness and affection was our way of life.
I love her dearly, dearly love her.
When my health changed, her love grew more,
She cared for me now with such tenderness and love.
She is there for me in sickness and in health,
Will hold me in her arms in death,
Thank God for wonder and love in marriage."

There were many such bad days. "Where is God when I need him the most?" I cried one night. How does God bring comfort to a sorrowing heart?

Comfort came through the presence and kindness of friends and family, through letters and messages of condolence from all over the world, from expressions of love and concern from those who shared our sorrow. It also came in many tangible ways like the friend who came with me to sort out all the official and legal matters. Through someone who sent me a very beautiful sari. Through friends from Singapore who sent me new tapes of music as listening to the old ones made me feel so sad.

Much comfort came from the Bible too. One particular verse kept coming not just to my mind, but also to my eyes in cards and letters that friends wrote.

"When you pass through the waters
I will be with you;
And when you pass through the rivers,
they will not sweep over you.
When you walk through the fire,
you will not be burned;
For I am the Lord, your God.

In acceptance lies peace. Kumar's lesson had to become real for me too. I had to embrace the loneliness, I had to accept the singleness of my life from now on, face the challenges and changes without anger and bitterness. Everyday was a constant battle with self-pity and the desolate feeling of loneliness. It was so easy to stay home and cry. Surely I was allowed to do that. It was so easy not to bother about anything at all. Why get dressed even, when there was no one to notice.

It was so easy to cut myself off from all aspects of love, to build a wall around myself so that I would not hurt so much. This way of life was numbing and effortless, but it brought no peace or joy. "Lord, please bring meaning into my life again. Take away this terrible loneliness. Grant me companionship and your peace," I prayed in desperation one dry.

"Certainly," came the answer, "but you will have to work at it…. Comfort others as you have been comforted, reach out in love as you have been loved, give as freely as you have received."

"But I need comforting myself," I argued, "The children have my arms around them when they cry, whom do I have? How can I possibly comfort someone else?"

A few days after I said that prayer, a friend lost her husband in a tragic accident. "You've walked in her shoes, you know what it feels like, so go to her," was the command.

A month later, another friend lost her husband. Comfort others as you have been comforted, reach out and touch as you have been touched, love as you have been loved.... following these timeless instructions has been the path out of the Valley of the Shadow of Death for me.

Just as dying was a positive experience for Kumar, a time when he was able to reach out to so many people and enrich their lives, and bring new meaning to them, grief was beginning to be a similar experience for me. I realized that my loss of Kumar was a call, not to sad weeping, but to a new day. To share our story with others in the same situation. To accept the inevitable changes and to continue being a witness.

Every death brings deep pain and grief, for it is a parting from a loved one. Death has the power to destroy, to tear apart, to devastate, to isolate. So does grief. Yet the message in Kumar's story is not about death and destruction, but of life and of something that is stronger than death and grief. Faith and love.

Faith gives the strength and courage to move on and face the challenges that bereavement brings. Faith, that in the larger scheme of things, God has a place for me, just as He had for Kumar. Faith too, to really believe that He is always with me, and will truly be my companion during the long lonely days ahead. For the boys too, faith was as important as love.

Love lives on in the hearts of those who love and are left behind. Death has no power over memories of kindness, of compassion, of joy, of caring and sharing. Grief is made bearable when we turn our hearts towards someone else, loneliness can be a pathway to God, and tears are the comforting assurance that God hears and feels our pain.

Thus a year after Kumar's death, Jamie was able to write,

"I am not alone
In this world so wide.
When you are torn apart and sad,
Raise your tear-filled eyes
And you will find
The reflection of your agony
In many more lives.

Thus it has helped me
To bear my loss,
Heavy though it was
With courage,
With a smile,
For his sake,
I've survived."

Although Kumar was not with us in the physical sense, his presence was still very much with us. His favourite flowers filled the room, the music that he so loved still flooded the house, the boys began reading his favourite psalms.

John too was able to write,

"I believe Appa is still with us, although we can't see him. I still feel close to him. Often I hear his voice in my heart saying, 'Don't cry, John-John, I love you son, I'm always with you.' I know that one day I will see him again."

I have come to look upon this change in my life as an Exodus, a leaving behind of the old--old comforts, old routines, old ways, and looking ahead and treading new wildernesses with hope and faith--that this period too will bring joy and fulfilment, just as being married did.

We moved out of the campus in Karigiri where we had lived for so many years and moved into the town and began a new way of life. I faced the challenges of doing things I had not done before..... seeing to the broken plumbing, mending the fuse in the middle of the night, going to the fish market, making all my decisions alone.

For the children too, it was a time of many changes. Jamie moved to a new school and took over much of Kumar's role in our lives. His protectiveness of me and the love and care he showed me were very touching. Often he would give up an evening with his friends to accompany me somewhere. Or he would sit and read through articles I had written with the same critical eye that Kumar had, and would give me ideas to work on. On All Souls Day he surprised us all by agreeing to read at the church service, a poem written by a bereaved son. Standing in the same place from where Kumar had read the Bible for so many years, he read,

"Accept my sadness as my prayer,
Watch with me please, and give me strength.
Accept my sadness; that is all I have now,
Give me hope,
Out of my mourning bring new life for me and
those I love."

Mallika celebrated her second birthday with great joy. She is a very lovely child, caring and sensitive. When John and I get a bit weepy, she brings a wooden spoon and says, "stop it," in exactly the same tone that I use when she whines. She has brought much love and joy and laughter into our lives again.

For John-John, the change has been the most difficult. He developed a stoic faith, and found comfort and meaning in doing things that his father once used to do for me, like bringing me my first cup of coffee in the morning. An injury to his eye due to an accident with a ball, left him sightless in one eye. Faced with the pain of operations, and the anguish of knowing that there will be many things that he could not do in the future, he bravely held my hand one night in hospital and said, "I'm going to beat this handicap, Amma." Kumar's spirit is very much alive in the children.

One of the changes I now face is learning to channel many of my needs as a woman, such as the need for touch, for hugs and affection, into something where it can take on a positive meaning. I still need a variety of loving relationships, and learning to love all kinds of people now by giving more of my time and my heart to those who are lonelier than me is a greater challenge than before.

Similarly, new directions at work, trying out different ideas, being a single parent and developing a constant loving relationship with my children, learning to rely on myself more in some situations, and asking for help in others, are all opportunities for personal growth.

For, it is a fact of life that the old order changes and gives way to the new. Everything turns. There is a time to live and a time to die, and a time for every purpose under heaven.

We could not have got through this period without the love and support of our families and our friends........ the many calls, the letters, the visits that made us feel very cherished. As a family we learned that love is indeed stronger than death, and that pain and sadness are redeemed only by faith and love.